Ancient Peoples and Places

THE GREEKS

IN IONIA AND THE EAST

General Editor

DR. GLYN DANIEL

Ancient Peoples and Places

THE GREEKS

IN IONIA AND THE EAST

J. M. Cook

76 PHOTOGRAPHS
46 LINE DRAWINGS
7 MAPS

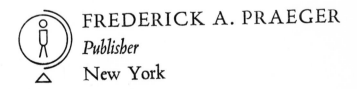

FREDERICK A. PRAEGER
Publisher
New York

THIS IS VOLUME THIRTY-ONE IN THE SERIES
Ancient Peoples and Places
GENERAL EDITOR: DR. GLYN DANIEL

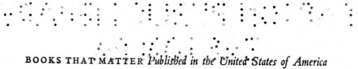

BOOKS THAT MATTER *Published in the United States of America
in 1963 by Frederick A. Praeger, Inc.
Publisher, 64 University Place
New York 3, N.Y.*
Library of Congress Catalog Card Number: 63-8041
*Printed in Great Britain by Hazell Watson & Viney Ltd.
Aylesbury and Slough*

CONTENTS

ILLUSTRATIONS

CHRONOLOGICAL TABLE

	BC
Fall of Hittite Empire	after 1200
Beginning of Iron Age in the Aegean	
Aeolic and Ionic Migrations	about 1000
Doric Settlement in South-east Aegean	
Foundation of Ionic League of 12 Cities ⎫	
Greek Settlement at Al Mina ⎬	8th century
Homeric Poems (*Iliad* and *Odyssey*) ⎭	
Cimmerian Invasions, Fall of Gordion and ⎫ Rise of Lydia	
City Planning at Smyrna	
Milesian Colonization in the North-east	
Ionic Guard formed in Egypt ⎬	7th century
Fall of Nineveh (612 BC), Rise of Median Empire	
Phocaeans in the West, Foundation of Massalia ⎭	
The Seven Sages	
First Samian Labyrinth begun	about 570
Anaximander of Miletus	
Greek Cities of Asia reduced by Croesus	after 561
Astyages the Mede overthrown by Cyrus the Persian	557/6 or 550
Great Temple of Artemis at Ephesus begun	
Croesus conquered by Cyrus	about 547
Greek Cities of Asia reduced by Harpagus	
Phocaean Victory off Corsica	
Persian Conquest of Egypt	525
Pythagoras in Italy	
Accession of Darius in Persia, Murder of Polycrates	522
Fall of Samos	
Darius' Conquests in Thrace and Indus Valley	
Heraclitus of Ephesus, Hecataeus of Miletus	
Burning of Sardis, Ionian Revolt	499

Foreword

THE HISTORY of the Eastern Greeks still remains to be
written. This little book is at best a pioneer sketch of such a
history; and inevitably it is coloured by the predilections and
prejudices of its author. But it does show that though our
knowledge of political and military events is too meagre to
yield a continuous narrative, there is no lack of evidence for the
social and cultural history of the Eastern Greeks.

The reader who perseveres to the end will perceive that the
subject of this book is really a double one. The earlier part is
concerned with the diverse fragments of the Greek people who
emigrated eastward to the coasts of Asia Minor after the end of
the Bronze Age and are known to us as the Eastern Greeks. We
shall follow them in the development of their civilisation; and
we may note the emergence of certain distinctive qualities of
character and intellect among them. But we must bear in mind
that they were never isolated from the Greeks of the Greek
mainland; the Aegean was always the focus of Greek civilisation; and, unlike their compatriots in Southern Italy and
Sicily, these Eastern Greeks were not in any sense colonials.

In the fourth century before Christ the centre of gravity of
the Greek world began to shift eastward; many Greeks emigrated to the new kingdoms of Alexander's East, and – as far
as concerns Greek history – what happened in the eastern half
of the Greek world mattered more than what happened in the
west. In the later chapters, therefore, where our subject is the
Greeks in the East, we shall find ourselves in mid-stream wit-
nessing the culmination of Greek achievement and the final
consolidation of civilised life.

Foreword

My thanks for doing out drawings go to R. V. Nicholls for Figs. 5, 19, 42, to Mrs M. E. Cox for Figs. 6, 18, 22, and to Mrs Sandra Macqueen for Figs. 7, 8, 10, 12, 14, 16, 26, 28, 31, 34, 44, 45, 53; for doing out the maps to H. A. Shelley. M. E. Weaver re,drew some figures. For permission to illustrate I am indebted to the British School at Athens for Figs. 4, 5, 19, 20, to the Ashmolean Museum for Fig. 6, to Akademie Verlag for Fig. 13, and to Verlag Gebr. Mann for Fig. 51. I have acknowledged the source of photographs that are not my own. For help in obtaining photographs I am indebted to R. M. Cook, D. E. L. Haynes and G. K. Jenkins.

Professor R. M. Cook and my elder son Michael were so good as to read through the text and give me the benefit of their sobering criticism. I admit that I have not always availed my, self of it. My wife has been a constant help, in particular by simulating the Thames & Hudson reader and also by reminding me of Alice's complaint, "What is the good of a book without pictures and conversations?" The pictures of course were part of the contract with the enterprising publishers and general editor of the series. But Alice's other demand is one that is not normally satisfied in books on Greek history. It may be ob, jected that some of the conversations and anecdotes that I have introduced are apocryphal and not true history. But I believe that they help to illuminate character and illustrate the creative imagination of the people who are the subject of the book. Fiction sometimes makes sounder history than fact.

J.M.C.

CHAPTER I

Western Asia Minor before the Greeks

MILETUS, THE SELF-STYLED 'First Foundation of
Ionia, Metropolis of numerous great cities in the Pontus
and Egypt and many other parts of the World', is now shrunk
to a mere village. Its harbours are dry land, and the visitor must
ascend one of the hills of the ancient sea-port if he wishes to
descry the Aegean shore. For here, as in the other gulfs of this
coast, the sea has receded from the ancient beaches. Aided by
man, who in past ages deforested the mountain slopes, the
rivers carried down the silt that has filled the bays. More than
2,000 years ago the Maeander was pressing forward its pointed
delta like a shaft aimed at Miletus, and the longshoremen of
Priene had to go to law to safeguard their rights of passage
through the narrows. Finally, by Christian times, Miletus had
become an inland port on a lake that the river had sealed off.
Subsequently, thanks to its river communication, it recovered
a little of its commercial prestige by the Frankish capitulations
of the fourteenth century; but unlike the marine life in the
dwindling lake, it could not adapt itself to the lack of salt water
and relapsed into insignificance. Ephesus too lost its harbour
and sank to the condition of a country town; and in modern
times even Smyrna, which had usurped the commerce of its
stranded rivals, was threatened with a similar decay until the
Turkish authorities diverted the Hermus to an older and more
distant bed in 1886.

Except in the extreme north, where the Troad forms an isolated bastion of regular outline, the long gulfs give the west
coast of Asia Minor its characteristic tortuous physiognomy.
Between these gulfs, the mountain ranges run out in long head-
lands; and coastwise communication is often difficult, so that
under suitable conditions the larger islands, which continue the

line of the mountain ridges, can take advantage of their situation and act as foci for the adjacent mainland shores. At the
ends of the coast this is the natural rôle of Lesbos and Rhodes,
though an international boundary prevents them from exercising it at the present day. In the central part of the coast, however, four long rivers – Caicus, Hermus, Cayster and Maeander
– flow westward from the interior between the mountain
ridges, and their flat-bottomed valleys provide easy communication between the coast and inner Anatolia; the rôle of Chios
and Samos has consequently been a more restricted one.

PREHISTORIC
TIMES

From the fourth millennium before Christ, when human
habitation seems to have commenced there, this coast was
poised between the civilisations of the Aegean and Anatolia.
It never formed a single cultural province. Troy and its neigh-
bourhood, being shielded from the interior by the highlands of
Ida, tended to face towards the Aegean; but the land of the
four river mouths tended rather to look inwards up the valleys,
while the tortured mountain land south of the Maeander was
still virtually uninhabited in prehistoric times. Before the
Greek migrations, which took place soon after the end of the
Bronze Age, the population of this coast seems in general not
to have been Greek-speaking. Admittedly, excavation has
shown that Mycenaean settlements had been planted in Rhodes,
Cos and other islands near the coast, while on the horn of the
Maeander gulf there was a Mycenaean walled settlement at

Fig. 1

Miletus in the Late Bronze Age; and, though the bulk of the
population may well have been Carian, there were probably
Achaean principalities in this corner of the Aegean. But the
region northward from the Maeander mouth lay outside the
main Mycenaean cultural sphere; and though the great city of
Troy evidently maintained strong commercial connections with
the Achaean world and may even have been inhabited by a
kindred people, this coast seems to have been only lightly
touched by Mycenaean culture.

Fig. 1. Late Mycenaean tankard found at Miletus; fish, water-birds and lilies

The cults of the coast in historical times are symptomatic of earlier relations. The incoming Greeks at the beginning of the Iron Age set up cults of their city goddess Athena on their citadels. But in the Troad and on the adjacent shores they continued at many points the worship of a native god identified with Apollo, while at the head of the Ionic gulfs to the south it was the old Anatolian goddess who continued to be venerated as the principal deity. It is no doubt this latter goddess whose colossal image, carved in a rock-niche at the foot of Mt Sipylus behind Smyrna, was already known to Homer as the petrified Niobe weeping for her children.

Plate 1

Homer in the eighth century BC sang of the siege of Troy by the Achaean heroes; and no doubt its capture, which (as we now believe) must have occurred before 1200 BC, was an important event in Late Bronze Age history. It is fortunate that the Greek tradition is so definite; for otherwise the archaeologists of the present day must inevitably attribute the destruction of Troy VII A to the Hittite king Tudhaliyas IV, who broke the Assuwan confederacy on this coast in the second half of the thirteenth century. Homer names Cilicians and Lelegians on the shores opposite Lesbos, and Carians in the south at Miletus; and we may, if we wish, apply these names to the old inhabitants of these lands. But he has nothing to say of inhabit-ants of the coast in between; the Greek cities were not yet founded in the time of the heroes, and in Homer this coast is a blank.

In legends transmitted by later Greek writers we hear of Amazons here, and of the city of Tantalus on Mt Sipylus. Modern scholars have variously suggested that the myths of the Amazons enshrine the memory of kilted Hittite warriors from the central Anatolian plateau, that Tantalus is the conquering king Tudhaliyas, or that Sipylus had its name from the war-like Hittite monarch Suppiluliumas. These things are possible, because the tablets of the Hittite kings seem to show that their armies penetrated more than once to the Aegean coast in the fourteenth and thirteenth centuries; and it may be that the pair of rock carvings, one of which still overlooks the road in the Karabel pass behind Smyrna, commemorated the passage of Tudhaliyas IV. On the other hand, some scholars prefer to suppose that the 'great king' who had these reliefs carved was a ruler of one of the western principalities that the Hittites could never permanently subdue. If this is the case, the principality might well be that Assuwa whose land Tudhaliyas destroyed; for, in early Greek literature, the name 'Asia', by which we denote a whole continent, seems to have belonged originally to the central region of this Aegean coastland. But theories of this sort belong to the realm of speculation. The one thing that we can say with some certainty is that in the era of collapse after 1200 BC, when kingdoms and palaces were ruined and inter-national relations were at an end, all centralised authority must have disappeared in the west of Asia Minor.

At Miletus a semblance of Mycenaean culture dragged on into the twelfth century; but, according to the latest reports of the excavators, the fortifications of the town were wrecked

Plate 2

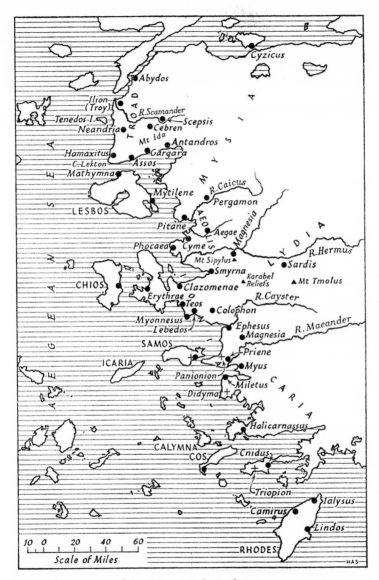

Fig. 2. *The West coast of Asia Minor in early Greek times*

beyond repair at the end of the Bronze Age. Apart from this, archaeologists cannot distinguish any relics of this epoch of disintegration on the coast; and the communities that survived must have been small and isolated. It was almost certainly to an underpopulated coastland, lacking in any effective political organisation, that the first Greek settlers came in their ships across the Aegean.

Chapter II

The Great Migrations and the Dark Age

THE PRIMARY Greek settlement of the west coast of Asia Minor belongs to the Dark Age which followed the collapse of the Late Bronze Age kingdoms. Painted pottery of the style called 'Protogeometric' has been found on six or seven different coastal sites in Ionia, and scraps of similar ware have also been reported by the American excavators at Sardis in the Lydian plain. Pottery of this sort is dated in the main to the tenth century, and its presence seems to prove that Greek settlement in Ionia was already well advanced in that century. Of the excavated sites, Miletus has yielded Protogeometric pottery in some quantity in the latest campaigns; and at Smyrna, where excavation was recently carried down through the earliest Greek strata by an Anglo-Turkish mission, more than one level of occupation with Protogeometric pottery came to light. Greek settlement at Smyrna may, on the present evidence, be reckoned as having begun as early as 1000 BC; at Miletus it may prove to have begun earlier.

IONIA
Fig. 2
Fig. 3

Fig. 3. Small vases from a grave in Southern Ionia

The foundation of the Ionic cities is described in the classical traditions, which are known to us now through late writers like Strabo and Pausanias but were first worked into systematic 'history' in the fifth century BC. The traditions present this movement as a massive migration across the Aegean: the main body of emigrants was 'the Ionians' – a people which had been driven out of its ancient homeland in the northern Peloponnese and settled temporarily in Athens; but the leadership was entrusted to Athenians and Pylians who had taken refuge in Athens (chief among them being the numerous cadet sons of King Codrus), and a variety of emigrants from Boeotia and other parts of Greece came to swell the ranks. In fact, the historical accuracy of these detailed traditions is suspect; the conception of the Ionians as a separate people is almost certainly an invention of the racial theorists, and we may suppose that few, if any, of the founders of the Ionic cities were genuine children of Codrus. Indeed, the actual process of settlement may have lasted for several generations. Nevertheless, some features of the traditional account are well founded. For instance, the movement was not so much colonisation as migration; the settlers were not linked to a mother-city by any official ties of filial piety, religious worship or social institutions, and from the outset they developed their own individual political organisms. In historical times many Ionians acknowledged a sentimental attachment to Athens as their parent city; and there were sufficient common elements in their religious cults and civic institutions to justify the belief that Athens had played the major part in sending out the settlers to Ionia. But the Ionians of the East were a mixed crowd, and it was only after crossing the Aegean that they acquired some sort of unity and developed the special characteristics that made them an exclusive people. In time they appropriated to themselves the name of 'Ionians', and in consequence the geographical term 'Ionia' is limited to their territory (or, at most, to that of themselves and their neighbours in the East Aegean). But we must bear in mind that these were not in fact the only Ionians – in its broader sense the name includes many islanders and even the Athenians. On the other hand, there appears to be no connection between this name and the sea that is called

'Ionian'; though they appear the same in English, the vowels are in fact quite different.

In historical times there were twelve cities of Ionia. Two of them (Chios and Samos) were on islands that lie close to the Asiatic shore. The other ten were on the mainland: they were, in their order along the coast from north to south, Phocaea and Clazomenae on the Gulf of Smyrna, Erythrae, Teos, Lebedos, Colophon (which lay nine miles inland), Ephesus by the mouth of the Cayster, and (in the gulf of the Maeander) Priene, Myus, Miletus. In the north of Ionia, Smyrna was by origin an Aeolic town, but at an early date it was captured by Ionians from Colophon; the story goes that these Ionians had come to Smyrna as exiles and been accepted by the Aeolic inhabitants, but took the opportunity of seizing the city while the citizens were out celebrating a festival of Dionysus. Smyrna was destroyed by the Lydians about 600 BC, and to Herodotus in the fifth century BC there were just twelve cities of Ionia. But we can hardly doubt that there had once been more of them. The diligent traveller at the present day can find traces of small nameless settlements on little peninsulas that jut out from the rugged Ionic coast-line; on some of them, sherds of pottery with painted geometrical decoration can be gathered on the surface or picked out of the bottom of sea-washed banks, and there is little doubt that the number of towns in the Ionia of the tenth and ninth centuries greatly exceeded the ten that ultimately apportioned the Ionic coast among themselves. A few of the major settlements, like Ephesus and Miletus, may have had a considerable population from the outset; but the majority seem to have been small, and some of the little peninsulas could not have housed more than a few dozen families.

Before considering the growth of these Ionic settlements we must turn to survey the other sectors of the coast. North of the River Hermus stretched Aeolic territory, with Cyme at the head of a bay where the main route down the coast turns inland along the north edge of the plain of the Hermus. Cyme occupied a pivotal position in the southern Aeolis and is said to have been the mothercity of many little Aeolic towns of the region – traces of some of these forgotten towns also can be discovered by the traveller. Herodotus, reciting his history in the fifth century B C, said that the Aeolians here once formed a league of twelve cities corresponding to the Ionic dodecapolis, but their number was reduced to eleven by the Ionic capture of Smyrna. With the single exception of one narrow mountain valley, up which lay the remote town of Aegae, these Aeolic settlements seem to have been strung out in ribbon development on either side of Cyme; half of them, set on crags that fringe the lower Hermus valley, stretched inland towards Magnesia, while the other half, planted on salient peninsulas, studded the coastline from Cyme northwards to Pitane beyond the mouth of the Caicus.

The fifthcentury writers attributed the Aeolic settlement in the northeastern Aegean to the posterity of Orestes, and there were Aeolic families there who claimed descent from Agamemnon. But these pedigrees inspire no greater confidence than those of the Scottish kings. We are told that in historical times these Aeolians acknowledged a kinship with the Boeotians of mainland Greece, and their speech was most closely connected with the dialects of Boeotia and Thessaly. It seems therefore likely that they came mainly from the eastern flanks of mainland Greece, their original homelands lying further north than those of the Ionians and having been less permeated by Mycenaean culture. As regards the beginnings of Aeolic settlement here, there is as yet no reliable archaeological evidence. But the Aeolic migration to the Asiatic coast probably dates to approximately the same era as the Ionic. It can hardly be appreciably later if Smyrna was originally one of these Aeolic cities; for in the earliest Greek strata there, alongside the painted pottery with geometrical patterns, there was found an abundance of monochrome pottery similar to that which was produced by the Aeolians in Lesbos.

The valley of the Caicus and the mountains to northward were occupied by an Anatolian race called Mysians. In general, they were an aboriginal people of the hill country who did not take easily to new ways of life; and until the times of the Roman emperors they preferred to live a rural life. But they also possessed the fertile coastal stretch north of Pitane; and it was probably not until about 400 B C that they made way for Mytilene to plant villages along their shore. They thus formed a barrier in early times, and the original Greek settlement of the coast seems to have gone no further north than Pitane.

The big Aeolic island of Lesbos lies in the crook of the Asiatic coast here. In historical times it was divided among five separate cities. Those in the desolate western part of the island were small and clung precariously to their independence. But Mathymna in the north was by no means unimportant, and Mytilene was always one of the wealthiest of Greek cities. Archaeological research has shown that in the Late Bronze Age there were two large settlements in the fertile eastern end of the island, and that they were abandoned or destroyed before the end of the Bronze Age. It is tempting to connect their eclipse with the rise of Mytilene and to suppose that Aeolian Greeks were already established there in the Late Bronze Age. There is of course no certainty in this view; but it is clear that the people of Mytilene absorbed the whole eastern part of Lesbos, and recent archaeological discoveries seem to show that they were already expanding on to the Asiatic mainland in the Dark Age.

The expansion of the Mytilenaeans must have been a bold achievement. The coast directly opposite their own shores was denied to them by the native Mysians; and in their search for agricultural land they ventured round the headland of Mt Ida (Cape Lekton) and planted a row of towns up the gentle

27

western shore of the bastion of Asia which bears the name of Troad – a countryside now largely given over to groves of valonia oak. The oldest of these little towns were established as early as the eighth century, for odd potsherds of that date can be picked up on their sites. They were set on crests of the escarpment that lines the beach, and they give the impression that the first Aeolic settlement there was hardly more than skin-deep. These Aeolic towns stopped short of the narrow point of the Dardanelles, Ilion (Troy) being the limit of their advance; beyond this lay the zone which the Ionians were destined to colonise. Before Mytilene surrendered to Athens in 427 BC, the towns of this coast were not independent cities but possessions of Mytilene.

The Troad is isolated from the habitable lands of Asia Minor by the massif of Ida and the broken mountain country lying to the east of it. The interior basin of the river Scamander is thus most easily approached from the west coast; and on its flanks several Aeolic cities came into being up country. The richest of them were Cebren and Scepsis, which had abundant grazing land and became flourishing wool-cities. On the south coast of the Troad conditions were very different. The sunny slopes of Ida fall steeply towards the sea, and water flows perennially from the mountain springs. The sheltered coast is now a continuous olive yard, but in antiquity it could yield several harvests in the year; Gargara, Virgil says, was amazed at its own crops. The Aeolic cities of this riviera west of Antandros were founded from Mathymna; but they enjoyed independence and a quiet prosperity on their rocky heights. Antandros itself seems to have been a native town in the seventh century and to have been annexed later by Mytilene.

The Aeolians will appear little in subsequent chapters of this book; and a word may be said of their qualities here. They occupied a fertile agricultural belt which was in the main backed by rough hill-country, and they had neither commerce nor contact with the native peoples of the interior. They thus enjoyed the blessings of a secluded life; and only Mytilene, from its sheer size, turned to commerce and was drawn into the currents of world affairs. On the evidence of their own actions and other people's views of them, the Aeolians seem to have been of a conservative temper, ready to brag though with no great stomach for action, and fond of the countryside and sensitive to the beauties of music and poetry – in their life and literature at the present day the Lesbians show similar qualities of keen appreciation.

To the south of Ionia, the coast was in the hands of the Carians. Little is known of their origins, though their language was still in common use in the fourth century BC. They were probably an old Aegean people and not Indo-European in speech; but they had absorbed a good deal of Mycenaean culture and were in constant and regular contact with the Greeks. The geographer Strabo tells us that they first earned the title 'barbarians', not because they talked a foreign language, but because they sounded so 'bar-bar-ous' when they talked Greek. After the end of the Bronze Age they spread over the southwestern part of Asia Minor, living the life of herdsmen in hilltop villages whose stone-built ruins defy time and the elements and still remain to be studied and planned.

CARIA AND DORIANS

Plates 3, 4

Some time around 900 BC Dorians appeared as new settlers in the islands of Rhodes and Cos that lie off the Carian coasts; and, after this, more Dorians settled on the peninsulas of western Caria. Two new Greek cities came into being at Cnidus and Halicarnassus; and Dorians seem also to have mixed with the native communities along the shores of the Carian gulfs. The east coast of the Aegean was thus divided into three parts, and each of the three main branches of the Greek race – Aeolians, Ionians and Dorians – had its own sector. The settlers at Cnidus were of Spartan extraction, but the remainder of the Dorian settlers in this region seem to have come from the Argolid. They were conscious of their racial unity as distinct from the Ionians; and five established Dorian cities celebrated their kinship in a joint festival of Apollo, which was held, with athletic contests, at Triopion near the Cnidian headland. The cities were Lindos, Ialysus and Camirus – the three cities of Dorian Rhodes – together with Cos and Cnidus. Herodotus insists that his own home town, Halicarnassus, had been a member of this union until it was expelled because of the unsportsmanlike behaviour of one of its athletes – he carried his prize home instead of dedicating it to the god; but it may be that in fact Halicarnassus did not rank as fully Dorian, and certainly its dialect seems to have been Ionic. In the south-east Aegean, as in Old Greece, the Dorians settled down as stolid farmers of the broad acres. They had little part in the cultural activity and traffic of ideas that accom-panied the Greek Renascence; and, as we shall see in a later chapter, it was only after the breakdown of the Athenian empire in the late fifth century that they began to adapt them-selves to new conditions of urban life and civilisation.

EARLY HISTORY OF IONIA

In the remainder of the present chapter we shall consider the Greeks of the central part of the coast, because our knowledge of the settlements in the Dark Age, whether it comes from literary sources or archaeological discoveries, is practically con-fined to Ionia. The Ionic cities, like many of the Aeolic ones also, were planted on peninsulas which were linked to the coast by a low isthmus. These situations were cool, and they were suitable for a maritime people. They also gave the shortest possible line of defence against any attack from the landward

Plate 5

side. Lebedos, one of the smaller Ionic cities, may serve as an illustration of such a peninsula projecting from a shelving coast-line; and another is the beetling rock of Myonnesus, whose

Plate 6

connecting causeway was so low that it has been submerged by a five-foot rise in sea level on this coast. In this we are reminded of the migration-settlement of the Phaeacians in the *Odyssey*:

there Odysseus is depicted as having to cross a slender cause-way, with boats drawn up on either side; and after that he pauses to admire the spectacular battlements of the fortification before entering the peninsula city. In the excavations at Smyrna such a wall circuit, dating to the ninth century, has come to light; it was more than once remodelled in the succeeding centuries.

Fig. 4

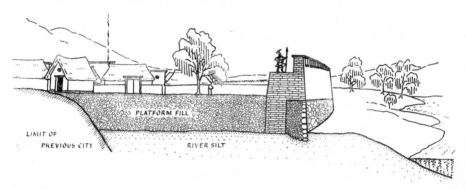

Fig. 4. Diagrammatic reconstruction of early Greek fortification at Old Smyrna, ninth century BC. (*Redrawn from* Annual of British School at Athens, *vol. 53–54*)

The houses of the citizens in the Dark Age seem to have been humble cottages. There may of course have been the occasional larger house, but in the main these cottages had no more than one small room, sometimes enlarged by a shallow porch at the front. The walls were made of sun-dried mud brick set on a low footing of rough stones; but since the roofs were of thatch, the houses were often built for convenience on an oval plan. The simple wooden framework of the roof will normally have been supported on poles, and a central hearth of clay provided for the needs of cooking and heating; the smoke could escape by an aperture under the end of the roof-ridge or by small vents along the top of the walls (both systems

Fig. 5

31

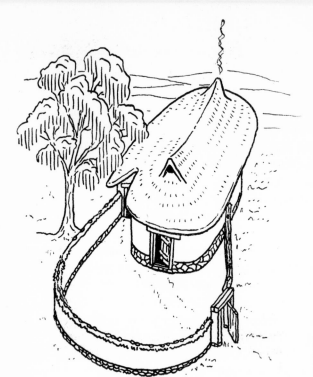

Fig. 5. Typical house of the Late Dark Age at Old Smyrna. (Drawing by R. V. Nicholls)

are known to us in miniature house-models of early times); but these cottages must nevertheless have been grimy, and they were small, dark and ill-appointed. In front of the cottage was a fenced yard, where geese or an animal might be kept; and some of the yards perhaps contained a circular granary partly sunk in the ground and lined with a stone wall. Miniature terracotta *Fig. 6* models of such 'beehive' granaries have been found in graves and may sometimes now be seen on museum shelves; some of them are labelled 'children's money boxes', but this explana-tion is out of the question because they date to the centuries before the invention of coinage. We hear of such a 'beehive' building in the yard of Odysseus' house in the *Odyssey*; it was evidently round its pointed roof-peak that Telemachus slung a cable when he made up his mind to hang the dishonoured serving-maids.

At Smyrna, where the peninsula was barely 400 yards long, the increase of population led to overcrowding in the eighth century. Before the end of that century, when a catastrophe of some sort occurred, there may have been 400–500 family cot, tages within the town walls; and the spaces between them were narrow and crooked. What had once been a roomy village site had turned into a slum town. Under such conditions the dan, ger of fire must have been always present; and we may apposite, ly call to mind Homer's simile of a fire raging through a town on a windy day and the thatched houses 'crumpling in a great blaze'. It is not improbable that conditions were better in some of the other Ionic cities. At Miletus the old excavations shed no clear light on the state of affairs in the Dark Age. But since this paragraph was first written the present German excavators have reported the discovery of traces of Dark Age walls, and especially of the corner of a sturdy house-footing which stood at least three courses high; this building seems to have been laid on a deliberately levelled patch of ground and was destroyed in a general conflagration that devastated this part of the town

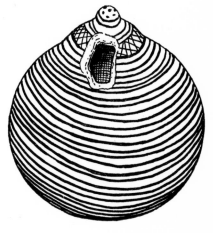

Fig. 6. Terracotta model of granary in the Ashmolean Museum, Oxford. Ht about 5 in. It is probably to be im, agined as mainly underground, with the trap-door above ground-level and the roof-peak supported by a central pole inside

in the eighth century. Certainly, if a covered stone drain found running alongside this house belongs to the same epoch, we may imagine that Miletus was better set up than Smyrna at the end of the Dark Age.

Apart from the overcrowding, the increase in population must have been welcome. Land was abundant before the Lydian kings set a limit to the Ionians' frontier in the early seventh century; and in early times the problem there, as in Jefferson's America, will not have been how to get the most out of the available land, but how to make the best use of the available labour. Despite the wretchedness of their town⁄ houses, the Greek settlers had substantial holdings of land; Aristotle tells us that in Colophon in early times the majority of the citizens had extensive properties, and some of the other cities seem to have had the use of native labour to work their land. Thus the number of Greeks on the coast of Asia was small; but they were able to enjoy a certain degree of leisure, and so they could give their minds more freely to cultural pursuits.

About 800 B C, or not much later, the Greek possession of the whole Ionic coast⁄line was complete; and it was perhaps then that a crystallisation took place in which ten cities of the coast, together with Samos, apportioned the whole land be⁄ tween them. The pretext for this action was a war which some of the leading Ionic cities declared against the recalcitrant people of Melia on the coast south of Ephesus; and it was prob⁄ ably on this occasion that a number of small Ionic settlements were absorbed by their more powerful neighbours. The princi⁄ pal sanctuary of Melia, dedicated to Poseidon of Helicon, was made into a federal sanctuary of the new alliance and re⁄named Panionion. After this, the Panionic league became an exclu⁄ sive confederation of the twelve Ionic cities, the island of Chios, as well as Samos, being included; but the union did not in any way restrict the independence of the individual cities. In the meantime, the two Magnesias seem to have come into being as centres of Greek settlement inland; the people of Colophon had extended their boundaries until they possessed a vast inland plain stretching almost to Smyrna; and Ephesus and Miletus advanced their boundaries up the river valleys 20 or 30 miles inland from the coast. The Ionic cities thus came to own an ample territory, and in time they were brought into close contact with the native peoples of the interior. Trouble lay ahead of them; but, for better or worse, they had ensured that Ionia would have a future.

CHAPTER III

Society in Early Ionia

ARCHAEOLOGY CANNOT TELL us much about the people themselves. And this chapter would be a barren one, were it not for one man – some scholars would say *two* men – through whose genius and humanity these dry bones can be made to live. The man was a professional singer (*aoidos*), and the author of two great epic poems called the *Iliad* and the *Odyssey*. The ancient world knew him as Homer, and for the most part believed that he came from Smyrna and taught in the island of Chios. In the *Iliad* he presented to his audience the complete scene of war; his immediate theme was the Anger of Achilles and its Results – not the least of which was this, that the long absence of Achilles from the battlefield left room for other, more civilised heroes in the centre of the action. The *Odyssey*, on the other hand, may be regarded as the poem of the Complete Man.

The two poems, in different degrees, were traditional; they enshrined that memory of Late Bronze Age heroes and heroic deeds which the Ionians had carried with them across the Aegean; and being full-length epics, they set in a final form much of the matter that generations of Ionic singers had been elaborating before Homer was born. The knowledge of the heroes – their stories, their lineage and their homes – was to some extent historical; such phenomena as kingship, or isolated single combats and the use of chariots in war, were essential elements of the old stories; and here and there we find the mention of an object or technique which seems to have its proper place in the Late Bronze Age. We must also bear in mind that the stories were being sung in poetic form by Ionic singers during the Dark Age, so that poetic skill had come to consist not only in invention but in the ability to remember and adapt.

Consequently there was much that was old in Homer, both in the narrative and in the language; and again, here and there in our text of the two poems there must be changes or additions made by later reciters who bridged the gap between Homer and the first written texts of his poems. Nevertheless, despite all this, there is so much that is consistent in the general make-up of the poems, there is so much that is taken for granted in the human and social background and so much that can be shown by archaeological discoveries to belong to Homer's own times, that (after due allowance has been made for anachronisms and traditional elements) we can with some confidence draw on the poems to illuminate the general pattern of life and thought in the Ionia of the poet's own day.

It is not, of course, universally agreed among present-day scholars that the *Iliad* and *Odyssey* are creations of a single poet; and it is just conceivable, perhaps, that the *Odyssey* is the creation of a second master. But the family likeness is in any case so close that we are bound to regard the two poems as products of the same milieu. Our *Iliad*, as a consciously created major epic, belongs to the eighth century: on the one hand, the mention of sacrifice to Poseidon Heliconius (the deity of Panionion), the conditions of city life and phenomena like temples, battle lines and four-horse racing chariots forbid us to date the poem earlier; and, on the other hand, it now seems clear that the mainland of Greece felt the impact of full-scale Ionic epic before 700 BC. Our *Odyssey* is a second Ionic creation of about this time; at the very latest, it might date to the early years of the seventh century. We may thus regard Homer as belonging in time to the end of the Dark Age, though the spiritual values he embodies are far from dark.

In Homer we find cities of the classical Greek type, with walls which enclose the whole urban population, and temples for public worship. Cities like this are something totally different from the Mycenaean citadels of Late Bronze Age Greece, and they imply a new conception of city life in which every citizen has his share. The houses of the gods on earth must also be new, because there is no archaeological evidence of temples in Greece before the eighth century. Kings are an essential part of the heroic stories, and kingship is therefore nearly always present in Homer. But the idea of citizenship is already well advanced in the poems, and government appears to function with a council of elders (*boule*) and a popular assembly (*agora*). In several passages it is clear that public opinion is a force that has to be taken into account. On the balance of all available evidence, it seems unlikely that there was much left of monarchy in the Ionic cities of Homer's own day; and it is also evident that at this time there was little scope there for the clans (*gene*) that are thought to have formed the basis of old-world society in mainland Greece.

In urban life there were specialists who worked for the community and were respected for their skill. Those mentioned as such by Homer are seers, doctors, carpenters, singers and heralds; and to the list of tradesmen we may add smiths and potters. There was evidently little fine silver and gold work produced in Ionia, and works of art in the precious metals are commonly described as the products of Sidonians from Phoenicia or of a god. Good masonry was admired by Homer, but it is not clear whether building had yet become a specialised trade; and leather-working, like weaving, may generally have been carried on in the home. An ivory worker is once mentioned, and furniture may occasionally have been inlaid with ivory in Dark Age Greece; but such work hardly appears in archaeological contexts before the seventh century, when Syrian and Phoenician trinkets began to make their appearance in Ionic sanctuaries. There was of course no coined money yet; and shopkeepers do not occur in Homer. While works of art form a subject for admiration, there are no artists in everyday life in the poems; and archaeology has revealed nothing more than plain craftsmanship in Dark Age Ionia. That is why the couple of drawings that accompany these paragraphs on Homeric life have had to be taken from Athenian vases, on which painted scenes are both frequent and finely executed. Without any doubt, the most skilled craft in eighth-century Ionia was that of the singers, who had developed a highly sophisticated art-form of their own; Homer was probably not enhancing his own status when he assigned to the singers an honoured place in society.

Sea-faring and fishing were everyday activities, though no fish course varied the menu of meat and red wine. In the poems trade is combined with piracy, and the latter seems to have been considered the more honourable profession of the two; but in Homer this may be a concession to the traditional heroic temper. Despite the martial tone of the epic, the poet's own feeling is that war is a senseless evil. At the same time, in an unguarded moment the goddess Athena professes herself game for a cattle-raiding expedition that would result in bloodshed.

Men work their fields and gardens; they irrigate the beds, though vegetables formed no regular part of traditional heroic diet. The herdsman's hardy life is frequently mentioned. The hills were no doubt more wooded than now; there was plenty of timber, and in the poems we find that wild boar, goat and deer are hunted. The breeding of horses is taken seriously and can even be a cause of war; dogs are bred for their appearance as well as for guarding flocks and hunting. The heroes at Troy do not normally perform menial tasks. But in everyday life in the poems we find men and women accustomed to manual labour even in the best families; and one of the qualities most admired in Odysseus is his ability to do things himself. Not only is he found charming by women, a father to his people and an admirable family man; not only is he a famous athlete, strong swimmer and crack shot; he can build a boat and a bedroom, dig trenches, lug the heaviest loads, tie up his own luggage, fumigate the house, and challenge younger men to a ploughing or scything match.

The Phaeacians, who seem to be very much to the poet's own taste, appear as notoriously fond of comfort, and their avowed interests are dancing and the guitar, hot baths, clean clothes and comfortable beds. Athletics and ball games are popular, and the parlour game is backgammon. Music is the universal entertainment, and we hear of the craze for the latest song. Festal banquets are enjoyed and vintage wine is appreciated. Women move so freely in Homeric society that we must assume that in the Ionic cities they led a much less restricted life than was forced on them in classical Athens; in Homer they are often self-willed and at times masterful – among the Phaeacians Odysseus had to summon up all his resources of ingenuity and tact to parry his hostess' searching questions and win her esteem.

In the stately homes that the epic tradition demanded, life was by no means ungracious; in contrast to classical Greece, people sat to their meals and lay down in comfort to make love. It is difficult to say whether marriages were often love-matches; but certainly a tender feeling often pervaded the life of married couples, and it was not necessarily a sign of a bad wife if (as Hector in a carefree moment protested) she fed her husband's horses before she fed him. In some ways human nature was much as it is now; girls were nearly always nice before they got married, and a white skin or a neat pair of ankles called for comment. For women there was scent and cosmetics, together with a wide range of jewellery; and goddesses at least knew a good deal about beautification. There must have been trade in such luxuries. The gods themselves relied on regular pigeon-convoys for their ambrosia, and we are told that one carrier was lost in every passage of the Clashing Rocks. Clothes, on the other hand, were not cut to the figure as they had been in the Late Bronze Age; Athena

Fig. 7

could put on her father's costume to go to the war, and if she then strutted like a pigeon, that is the gait of a goddess when armed for battle.

Religion in Ionia was of a different character from that of mainland Greece. Torn away by the roots, the Ionians had lost their religious attachment to the spirits and cults of their old homelands. The gods of Homer are the Olympians, whose universal abode is among the clouds. In this divine family Zeus is first in strength and right of primogeniture; and in the last resort he is acknowledged to be omnipotent. It is often said

Fig. 7. Maidens in a dance, from an Athenian vase found in a grave near Athens.
By the Analatos Painter, about 700 BC

that in the *Iliad* even Zeus is subject to a power called Moira (Destiny) in whose ultimate control of human ends Homer himself believed. But, broadly speaking, this seems to be an illusion. It is true that Zeus cannot prevent the fall of Troy. But Moira here is the epic tradition, or (if we like) History. Troy actually fell; and therefore, whether Zeus likes it or not, it has to fall. No wonder the goddesses get so angry on the golden floor when Zeus mischievously suggests that Hector or Sarpedon should be rescued from his fate: 'the man', they complain, 'was long ago destined to his doom.' This foreknowledge of history is occasionally imparted to mortal men, so that Hector and Achilles foresee their own fate; and the poet is thus able to invest his highspirited heroes with a lingering aura of fatalism that sharpens the dramatic tension.

Whether in their arguments on Olympus or in their dealings with human beings, the gods of the *Iliad* are curiously lacking in better feelings, and lacking even in moral principle. They cannot often be held to set a noble example to mankind by their conduct, and almost every one of them is at one time or another made to appear ridiculous. The divine scenes in the *Iliad* are generally introduced either as amusing interludes or as a machinery to precipitate the action; and the gods are reflections of human nature and human relationships. It is difficult to believe – though many scholars do somehow believe it – that Homer's brilliant, cynical treatment of his gods can really have concealed any deep religious conviction. His belief was in man, not in gods. In his universe, faith – in the sense of religious faith – is lacking; but there is hope in this world, and charity abounds.

Homer's faith in man is the cornerstone of Ionic humanism. Man must be prepared for anything that may befall. The best man is the one who, unaided, can do anything that is required of him, handle any situation by word or action, and endure all things; he should be courteous, quickwitted and missing no cues, and at the same time steady in mind and judgement. These are the qualities that made up the character of Odysseus, which later generations of Greeks never quite managed to comprehend. Morality and religion to Homer are two separate things. The citizen must do his duty to his city, the strong must help the weak and unfortunate, and the leader must look after those who are in his charge – that is why as early as the sixth line of the *Odyssey* Homer felt obliged to explain that it was through no fault of his own that Odysseus arrived back in Ithaca without his men; but it is not divine law that enjoins such conduct, it is man's own feelings of self respect or honour (*aidōs*). This, above all, is the reason why Homer remained for many centuries the foundation of Greek education, and why severe moralists like Plato despaired of him. If we do not believe that the Ionians can have been as humane and enlightened as this in the eighth century, we can only echo Pro fessor Stanford's phrase about Homer's morality, that 'after all, this is the characteristic quality of transcendent genius, to give beyond its conscious powers.'

There is much in Homer that foreshadows the later develop-ments of the Ionic genius, and not least his interest in the world around him and his curiosity about the cities and mentality of strange peoples. But we shall see the results of this desire for knowledge in the chapters that follow; what chiefly concerns us at this point is human relationships in early Ionia.

The Homeric epic being a cultured product, imagination and insight have gone into the distinction of personalities. Agamemnon, for instance, can never rise superior to jealousy; he comes in with his grievance at the beginning of the *Iliad*; and he is nursing his final grievance when he makes his last bow in the twenty-fourth book of the *Odyssey*. Menelaus in the *Iliad* is thoughtless, mostly ineffective, and sometimes foolish. In the *Odyssey* he reappears, older, but still bustling, and losing his temper with his butler; he talks of sacking one of his own cities to make a new realm for Odysseus, and he offers Tele-

Fig. 8

Fig. 8. Menelaus, or a companion, on an Athenian vase-stand from Aegina. Painter of the Eleusis Polyphemus Vase, about 670 BC

43

machus presents that are quite unsuitable for his rocky home. Nestor of Pylos is a very different character. Though old age has made him garrulous, he has understanding and a fine old-fashioned courtesy; it is he who spots the goddess when she arrives in disguise. His sons too have learned manners and tact in their father's house. There are few more exquisite scenes in Greek literature than that in which Antilochus makes amends to Menelaus after edging him off the track in a chariot race; and none shows the subtlety of Homeric conversation more clearly than the short speech made by Nestor's youngest son, Pisistratus, at Sparta.

Pisistratus had driven over with Telemachus from Pylos. After a bath and a bite of food they are recognised by Helen, and the talk presently centres on Telemachus' father, the lost Odysseus. Soon the whole party is prostrate with grief. Even Argive Helen is dissolved in tears. The young Pisistratus is the first to recover his poise, and he addresses Menelaus: 'Son of Atreus, the old man Nestor constantly says that you above all men are sensible, when we talk about you at home and ask each other questions. And now,' – as he fumbles for the right words – 'if I may make the suggestion, I don't enjoy lamenting after supper; and besides, dawn will soon be upon us. Not that I grudge anyone his right to weep for the dead and gone. This is the one thing we can do for them, to cut our hair short and let the tears run down our cheeks. For I too lost a brother who was far from being the meanest among the Argives – but you of course should know of him, though I never set eyes on him myself; for people say that Antilochus was beyond compare, both as a fast runner and as a fighter.' This speech recalls Menelaus to his duties as a host; a few complimentary words are said about Nestor and his sons, supper is served, and the conversation then turns to cheerful reminiscences. Theoretically we cannot be sure that Pisistratus knew of the incident in the chariot race at Troy; he makes no mention of his brother's skill with horses, and Menelaus studiously avoids all mention of Antilochus in his reply. But attention has been distracted from Telemachus' loss; a proper social atmosphere has been re-established, and even Odysseus could not have enquired more tactfully about the evening meal.

The many timely and delicate speeches in Homer are the clearest proof of Ionic sophistication. Humour is never far away. Teasing is frequent, but it is not often unkind (except of course on Olympus); and if we wish for proof of the subtle adjustment of social life in early Ionia, we shall find it in the misunderstandings to which so many Homeric scholars are even now prone. In the chapters that follow we shall not see the Ionic character again in such sharp focus; and if we could, we should probably not find it quite so attractive.

CHAPTER IV

The Expansion of Ionia

THE SUBJECT of this chapter and the next one is the expansion of Ionia to its full stature in the Mediterranean world; and in Chapters VI–VII we shall be concerned with the corresponding growth of the Ionic cities at home. This expansion proceeded so rapidly and on such a scale that it marks a new era, to which we may give the name 'Ionic Renascence'. It may be said to commence about the beginning of the seventh century. The end of a Renascence is more difficult to define; but we shall, for convenience, carry the story in these four chapters down to about 560 BC, when the Lydian king Croesus began to establish his supremacy over the whole coast.

EASTERN
NEIGHBOURS

Plate 7

Fig. 9

The American excavators at Sardis are now penetrating into levels of occupation of the Dark Age; and it seems almost certain that this sprawling town, whose citadel was perched on one of the crumbling rock-pinnacles that line the southern edge of the Lydian plain, will prove to have been the one important centre in the region at that time. So long as the so-called 'Heraclid' dynasty reigned there, Sardis does not seem to have been the capital of a politically powerful kingdom. The Ionic cities were able to advance their frontier deep inland; and the great power that the Greeks knew, or heard of, was that of the Phrygians on the plateau a couple of hundred miles to the east of Sardis. The Phrygians were said to have entered Asia Minor from Thrace; and, like the Thracians across the Sea of Marmara, they were beer-drinkers in historical times. Scholars have therefore assumed that they penetrated central Asia Minor from the north-west, coming across from Europe in the movement of peoples that took place about 1200 BC. But their origins are nevertheless perplexing. The first unmistakable evidence of Phrygian culture is large, brightly painted pottery vessels whose

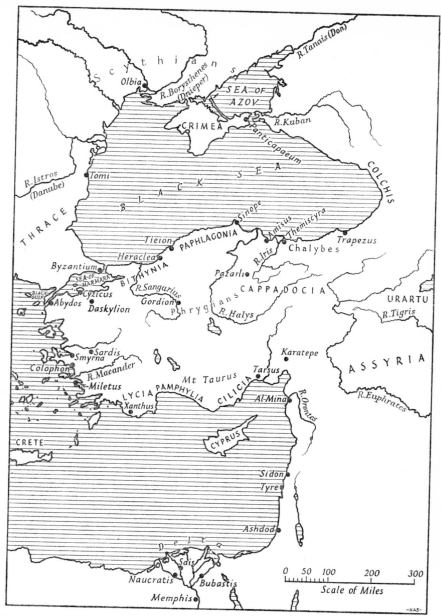

Fig. 9. Ionia and the Eastern World

Fig. 10. Painted panel decoration from an East Phrygian crater; found at Aliṣar, now in the Ankara Museum. Eighth century BC

Fig. 10   signature pattern is windswept geometrical stags in a hail-storm of concentric circles: this ware, however, does not seem to have been current before the eighth century; and, curiously, it makes its first appearance in the eastern citadels on the Halys river before penetrating to western Phrygia in the late eighth century. The earlier stages of what is presumably the Phrygian culture in western Phrygia are characterised by gray mono-chrome ware; at the moment this is very obscure, but light may be thrown on it when the American excavations at the capital city of Gordion on the Sangarius are carried down below the palatial stratum of about 700 BC.

The Anatolian plateau was not only rich in flocks but in timber also; and at the end of the eighth century the Phrygian princes in the city of Gordion lived in spacious half-timbered halls with first-floor galleries. They appreciated good metal-work and carpentry and possessed a local school of ivory carv-ing. The rulers were buried with lavish furnishings in wooden cabins covered by gigantic tumuli. They maintained some sort of direct contact with the East, because the arts of Assyria and the kingdom of Urartu (Ararat) are represented by handsome vessels discovered in these tombs. Curiously, there is no sign of similar contacts with the West; for no objects of Greek manufacture found at Gordion are dated earlier than about 650 BC. But here the negative evidence may be misleading. It seems likely that the Ionians had come to know and appreciate Phrygian craftsmanship a generation or two earlier; before the end of the eighth century the Phrygians had received the

Semitic alphabet in what at the moment we suppose to be a Greek form; and later Greek writers also said that a Phrygian Midas had married a princess of Aeolic Cyme. Finally, a wonderful chair, shown to Herodotus at Delphi, was said to be the judgement seat of Midas, dedicated to Apollo by the famous king of that name; and if the information was correct the chair must have been sent there about 700 B C. It was prob/ ably adorned with precious metals and carved ivory plaques, but the woodwork also will have had elaborate carving, to judge by the patterns on screens which the excavators of Gordion found in the great tumulus there in 1957.

Plate 8

The American excavators have suggested that this huge tumulus was the burial place of the great Midas' father, who died somewhere around 720 B C. Midas himself seems to figure in the Assyrian archives in the last decade or so of the eighth century, and he was evidently a troublesome neighbour for a short time. But at this juncture there appeared a more serious menace to the peace of the civilised Orient. This was a people who spread terror far and wide. From the Greek form of their name we know them as 'Cimmerians', and from the Book of Genesis as 'Gomer'; their memory probably survives in the place/name Crimea, and it may not be accident that the Georgian word for 'hero' is virtually identical with the As/ syrian form of their name ('Gimirri'). Driven from the Asiatic steppes by nomadic Scythians, these Cimmerians crossed the Caucasus and descended with their wagon trains into eastern Asia Minor. In the main they seem to have occupied Cappado/ cia between the Euphrates and the Halys river. But they spread devastation over much of the Near East; and in the early years of the seventh century they overwhelmed Gordion, where King Midas, according to a whimsical Greek legend, took his own life by drinking bull's blood. The Cimmerians continued their raids for half a century and more; and some of the Greek cities in the west suffered at their hands. But vexatious as these incursions were at the time, the damage did not prove lasting; and even the town of Gordion quickly regained its prosperity. There was, however, one momentous consequence of the sack of Gordion; with Midas' overthrow, the power of the Phrygian kingdom was permanently impaired, and the political initiative in Asia Minor passed out of Phrygian hands.

At this time the Heraclid line at Sardis was succeeded by the new dynasty of Gyges the Mermnad. The circumstances that surrounded this change of rulers are open to dispute because more than one account of the event was later current among the Greeks. In the better known story, which Herodotus relates, the queen's honour could only be satisfied by the death of her husband because he had smuggled Gyges into the royal bed-chamber to admire her beauty unseen; and this may possibly have been the official version by which the lovers sought to justify a less involuntary intrigue. For the implication was that if Gyges wished to live he must consent to reign. The new king combined political ambition with a warlike temperament; and under his vigorous rule Lydia became the leading power in Asia Minor. He captured Magnesia in the Lydian plain; further west, he attacked Smyrna and is said to have had some temporary success at Colophon. It seems as though he and his immediate successors were not yet strong enough to overrun the Greek cities of the coast, and they were probably content to make destructive raids in the harvesting season; but they effectively checked the forward movement of the Ionians, and from the Lydian plain at Sardis they had their choice of routes by which to swoop down on the Ionic coast.

IONIC COLONISA- TION IN THE NORTH-EAST

With their landward frontier thus blocked, the Ionians turned to overseas expansion. The cities of Lesbos had begun to plant settlements on both sides of the entry to the Dardanelles and on the 'Black Gulf' to the north of the Gallipoli peninsula; and several Northern Ionic cities began to take an interest in the Thracian coast, from which they could obtain wine, silver and slaves. But the most impressive achievement of all was that of the Southern Ionic city of Miletus. Situated on the tip of a stony promontory, with no convenient land route to the Maeander valley, the Milesians must always have kept up a brisk coastal and ferry traffic; and in early times this enterprising people acquired territory across their gulf and in the lower Maeander plain. In due course they occupied the small islands which lay to the west of their coast-line; and in the early seventh century they began their career of colonisation in the North-east. Miletus was later said to have been the mother of ninety colonies in the different seas. It is difficult to believe that she had the manpower to people so many cities single-handed. And we may rather think of her as the leader in a broader movement of overseas expansion. Miletus herself will have pro-vided 'oecists' (founders), shipping, and the requisite know-ledge of sea-routes and local conditions; but other Ionic cities must have provided a good proportion of the emigrants. This Milesian colonisation began with the penetration of the nar-rows of the Dardanelles, where Abydos was planted in the key position on the Asiatic coast; and it then proceeded along the southern shore of the Sea of Marmara (Propontis). The most successful, if not also the earliest, of the Milesian colonies here was Cyzicus by the end of the long tunny-fish run from the Sea of Azov. Up to the present time, archaeological discoveries do not offer any evidence of Greek settlement earlier than the late seventh century at Cyzicus; but excavations have recently been begun by Turkish scholars on the shore of the lake twenty miles inland, and they show that there was already an Ionic settlement in the early seventh century at Daskylion, where the Persian satraps of Phrygia later had their seat. Founded in territory that was presumably Mysian at the time, Cyzicus had a good hinterland to develop, and its electrum coinage became widely current in the North-east in the sixth century.

Fig. 11. Electrum stater of the Cyzicus mint; Heracles attacking with club and bow, tunny fish. 500–480 BC

Fig. 11

These northerly shores were bleak and wintry by Greek

standards; and so long as sunnier coasts were still open to their rivals, the Milesians might hope to keep a monopoly in this sphere of colonisation. But the Greeks had not been standing still. The states of Old Greece had felt the need of more land while the Ionians still had an expanding frontier; and waves of emigrants had sailed to the West from the harbours of Euboea and the Peloponnese. Sicily and southern Italy had thus become colonial preserves in the second half of the eighth century. The organised kingdoms of the Levant and Egypt might welcome traders, but they had no desire for foreign colonists. And consequently, by the seventh century, the North-east was the only undeveloped maritime area of any size that remained within easy reach of the Greeks. The Dorians of Megara on the Greek mainland still needed more space overseas; and about the middle of the seventh century they entered into competition with the Ionians by planting a group of colonies at the eastern end of the Sea of Marmara. These foundations, of which the most successful was Byzantium at the entry to the Bosporus, were later to act as pilots in the Megarian advance into the Black Sea. But the Ionians were well ahead. About the time that Byzantium was founded, if not even earlier, the Milesians worked their way up the currents of the Bosporus; and having thus forced the second and more difficult of the north-east passages, they began to plant a long trail of colonies along the Black Sea shore.

The ancient writers have left us no systematic account of the colonisation of the Black Sea, and the few dates that they provide for individual settlements carry no great conviction. Eusebius, who was bishop of Caesarea in the fourth century after Christ, gives a curiously divergent date (756 BC) for the foundation of Trapezus, which was itself said to be a daughter city of Sinope. This had led many modern historians to believe that the Ionic colonisation of Sinope and Trapezus was very ancient, and economic objectives have been postulated to ac-

count for this Dark Age enterprise – for instance, the importa-
tion of the high-grade iron of the Chalybes, and the gold of
Colchis which romantic scholars find symbolized in the story
of Jason and his sheepskin. But there is no evidence to support
such theories, nor even any connection with Colchis in the
early Argonaut legend; and it is inherently improbable that
trade with the most distant shores of the Black Sea would have
preceded the exploration of the Marmara. It may well be that
in the eighth century the Ionians heard talk of tribes and
curiosities of the Black Sea, and indeed Homer has some vague
knowledge of its southern coast. But first-hand acquaintance
with the great inland sea seems only to have come in the seventh
century when Greek poets for the first time talk of the Istros
(Danube), the Borysthenes (Dnieper) and the savages of the
Salmydessian coast, and when the name Istrocles ('called after
the Istros') was given to a child in one of the cities of Ionia.

Fig. 12

*Fig. 12. Painted signature on rim of Ionic bowl found at Old Smyrna: 'Istrokleës
(made me?)'. Probably about 630 BC*

Because of its size the Ionians called this sea 'Pontus' (i.e. 'open
sea')—it was their Main; and, along with Apollo the Leader,
the Homeric hero Achilles somehow received worship as a
patron deity along its north-western shores.

It is hardly accidental that the first sure signs of familiarity
with the Black Sea concern its European shores around the
Danube and Dnieper mouths. It is precisely this region that
shows the first visible signs of Greek penetration; and though

the earliest settlements may initially have been mere trading stations frequented during the summer season, it seems certain that the Ionians were establishing themselves as permanent resi‚ dents here in the second half of the seventh century. The dreary Scythian coast was not favourable to the Greek way of life; and centuries later, in the decay of Greek civilisation on these shores, Ovid regarded his banishment to Tomi as a fate grim‚ mer than death – though at that time Paris or Vienna would have been infinitely worse. But the Ionic colonisation of the Black Sea is historically important, and not merely as an outlet for surplus population. Within a century of its commencement the whole European coast as far east as the Crimea and the Kuban river had been studded with Greek towns which served both as trading posts and agricultural settlements. With the expansion of commerce in the Greek world, the new colonies were able to supply Greece with commodities, and merchant seamen with regular employment. Salted fish and hides were exported, and the grain of South Russia was shipped to Greece in quantity. Some of the Ionic colonies became substantial cities; industries were developed, and Olbia, most northerly of the Black Sea ports and the greatest market for the export of grain, adopted a regular town‚planning scheme about 500 B C. While fine wines, oil, textiles and works of delicate Greek craftsmanship were imported from the manufacturing centres of the Aegean, fruit trees and vines were successfully planted – especially in the Crimea; and local work‚ shops produced jewellery designed for the Scythian market or as presents for native chieftains.

Fig. 13
Plate 10

The Royal Scythian barrows have yielded, and are yielding, many treasures of Greek craftsmanship; and, curiously, the earliest examples of imported Ionic vases are often found many days' journey up‚country. The grain trade led Ionic settlers up the river valleys. As they mixed with the natives, half‚breed village communities came into being; the cults of native gods

Fig. 13. Designs on a fragmentary silver drinking-horn (rhyton), discovered in a chieftain's burial mound at Kelermes 200 miles up the Kuban River; excavated in the winter 1903–4 but only recently put together. East Greek workmanship of first half of the sixth century BC, but made for use by the Scythian tribal aristocracy.
(From J. Irmscher and D. B. Schelov, Griechische Städte und einheimische Völker des Schwarzmeergebietes*)*

Plate 31

were assimilated in the pattern of Greek worship; and, with increasing knowledge, the imagination of the Greeks was stimulated by accounts of the religious beliefs and folklore of distant tribes of the steppes and the eastern European forests. Among the fairy/tale figures that Ionic artists liked to depict is the Arimaspian driving off with the gold that the griffins guarded. On their side, the Scythians gradually evolved a somewhat abstract art/style which assimilated the para/ phernalia of the Greek bestiary. Outside the Crimea they re/ tained their nomadic habits and tribal way of life until about the third century B C; but many no doubt were sold down the river as slaves, and increasing numbers of Scythians (and later of Sarmatians) settled in the cities and were absorbed in the Greek world.

On the southern or Asiatic coast of the Black Sea there has up till now been very little archaeological exploration. Sinope, founded by the Milesians, was the earliest Greek colony on this coast; and its foundation might go back into the late seventh century, though nothing yet found there is older than the begin/ ning of the sixth. This coast presented a very different aspect from the Scythian one. The northern border of Asia Minor is a belt of mountain ridges that rise to 10,000 feet in the east and are aligned in successive ranks behind the coast. The shore/line runs in long straight stretches which often fall precipitously to the sea, so that harbours are few and far between. Apart from the Halys and the Sangarius, the rivers rise within the mountain belt and tend to flow parallel to the coast; there is thus little direct communication with the central Anatolian plateau, and this coast is for the most part isolated. In early times the maritime belt was inhabited by savage tribes, like the tattooed Mossynoeci who baked chestnut bread and fattened up their kings in hill/top turrets of wood. With a rainfall of forty inches or more in the year, the highlands had good forests of timber, and vines, olives, apple, cherry and nut trees grew on the lower slopes; the country was also celebrated for its drugs and poisons. In their journey from the breeding grounds in the chill sea of Azov, the young tunnies passed along the whole length of this coast. But east of the Milesian colony of Sinope the fishing was not so good; for it was only at this stage in their course that they were coming to maturity.

Sinope, the Queen of the Pontus, was founded in a sheltered nook on the eastern promontory of the Paphlagonian shore which lies opposite the Crimea. This is the waist of the Black Sea; and Strabo claimed that in clear weather both coasts were visible simultaneously from a ship in mid passage – the distance is in fact well over 150 land miles. Sinope was thus the best port for the crossing of the Black Sea, and from the fourth century onward its interest in the cross-trade is demonstrated by handles of oil jars with Sinopic stamps which have been discovered at Olbia and Panticapaeum. Its principal products were hardwood for furniture and salted tunny; but it also exported to Greece the steel of the Chalybes and Cappadocian miltos (red ochre or ruddle) from far up the Halys river.

Sinope was the mother city of several small colonies, of which the most easterly was Trapezus, named after its table mountain; properly speaking, these were not independent cities but paid a regular tribute to Sinope. The colonies won the friendship of the native tribes in their vicinity and acted as centres for their trade; but the hill tribes in between retained their savage customs and were of a hostile disposition when the Ten Thousand passed this way in 400 BC. The mouth of the Halys lay east of Sinope; and further east still lay another great delta of a river which in later times was known as the Iris but perhaps once had the outlet and name of the Thermodon. It was on the Thermodon that according to Greek mythology the trousered Amazons had the headquarters of their militaristic polity in the walled city of Themiscyra.

In the sixth century the monopoly of Sinope on this coast

Fig. 14.
Designs on architec-
tural reliefs in
terracotta, found
at Pazarlı in
Phrygia,
now in the Ankara
Museum.
Phrygian under
Greek influence,
sixth century BC

was punctured by a new foundation, Amisus (now Samsun), which was planted – apparently by a joint effort of Miletus and Phocaea – between the deltas of the Halys and Thermo-don. Amisus became the principal competitor of Sinope in traffic with Cappadocia; and the cities of this coast helped to transmit to the Phrygians of the interior that knowledge of Greek artistic motifs and techniques which, for instance, prompted the manufacture of the sixth-century terracotta relief-plaques of Pazarlı. The east end of the Black Sea also in due course received a Milesian settlement or two, which had little place in the history of the ancient world but brought the rudi-ments of Greek civilisation and economy to the natives of further Colchis.

The Ionic 'Main' received its name 'Black Sea' from the Slavs. In ancient times it was called Euxine ('Hospitable'), but this was a flattering reversal of its older Greek name 'Inhospit-able' (Axeinos). Scholars seek to connect the name Axeinos with old Semitic or Iranian words meaning 'dark,' 'north' and so forth, and deny that it is of Greek origin. But the epithet 'inhospitable' could not have been better chosen. The mariner who had wormed his way up the Bosporus would have the dangerous Salmydessian shore on his left hand; and on his right, along the barbary coast of Bithynia and Paphlagonia, there was no good shelter before Sinope 350 miles away. The interval on this side was presently narrowed by the placing of a small Milesian settlement at Tieion; but the anchorage there was not a safe one, and it was only when Heraclea assumed a place as one of the principal cities of this coast that a secure and unmolested harbour became available. This Heraclea, dis-tinguished by the epithet Pontica, was founded in the mid-sixth century by the people of Megara, but Boeotians helped to swell their ranks. It was primarily an agricultural colony; and when the native tribe of Mariandyni had been reduced to semi-slavery, Heraclea enjoyed the possession of an extensive territory and was able, like Sinope, to maintain its own fleet. It planted a colony or two in its own right at the western end of the Black Sea; and with these newest settlements the Pontic colonisation was complete.

Greek colonisation in the Western Mediterranean hardly falls within the scope of this book. But a word must be said of the mariners of Phocaea. This little city, the most northerly of the Ionic Twelve, had been founded by courtesy of Aeolic Cyme on the headland that forms the northern entry point of the Gulf of Smyrna. Phocaea lacked good arable land, and its population can never have reached five figures. But the Phocaeans had the benefit of a magnificent harbour; and when they took to seafaring, they quickly became the hardiest of Greek sailors. They knew their way about all the seas. But the one which they made peculiarly their own was that between Etruria and Spain. About 600 BC they founded a colony at Massalia (Marseille), which was later to become one of the leading cities of the ancient world; and the shore of the gulf from Heracles of the 'Lone Abode' (Monaco) to the 'Mart' (Ampurias) was in due course studded with little Phocaean settlements. The goddess who presided over this coast was Ephesian Artemis. Here, as in South Russia, a great river flowing from the north acted in the first instance as the artery for trade up-country; in the sixth century the chieftains of central Gaul were learning to appreciate Greek craftsmanship, and some of the grandest examples of the Greek bronze-smiths' art have been found as far afield as Burgundy and the Loire.

PHOCAEANS IN THE WEST

Fig. 22

Before this, perhaps about 620 BC, the Phocaeans had passed outside the Straits of Gibraltar to Tartessus (by Cadiz) and there won for themselves a monopoly in a market that probably handled tin and good bronze. It seems also, to judge by the presence of Greek place-names, that the Ionians may have succeeded in planting settlements at an early date on the African coasts, both in the Western Mediterranean and in the Atlantic;

but if so they were not long-lived. It is at first sight peculiar that the Phocaeans, as Herodotus reports, did not sail in merchantmen but in fifty-oared war galleys; for in normal circumstances the enormous reduction in cargo space would not have been compensated by the chance profits of privateering. But in the Western Mediterranean abnormal conditions prevailed. With the foundation of Carthage about the end of the eighth century, the Phoenicians had gained a firm footing in western waters. Their 'New City' (in Phoenician 'Kart-Hadasht') was engaged in building up its power in the seventh century and presently drove the Greeks out of their stations and markets in the Far West. In their fast warships the Phocaeans kept up the competition for many years on the Punic Main, and finally by a supreme effort they defeated the combined Carthaginian and Etruscan fleets in a battle of annihilation off Corsica about 535 B C. But the Phocaeans were not a numerous people. Their own losses in the battle were so heavy as to prove irreplaceable; so Carthage duly established her monopoly of the tin trade and of traffic on the West African coast, and thereafter the limits of the Greek world were in Sicily and the north-east coast of the Spanish Peninsula.

CHAPTER V

Greeks and the Levant

THE SOUTH COAST of Asia Minor resembles the north coast in one important respect, that high mountains rise steeply from the sea, denying access to the interior. There are only two regions here which readily invite settlement. The first is the Pamphylian plain at the head of the Gulf of Attalia (Antalya); the second is at the east end of this coast where the Taurus veers away north-eastward from the Cilician shore. This Cilician plain had attracted emigrants from the Aegean in the Late Bronze Age when the Hittite Empire was on the verge of collapse about 1200 BC; and the discovery of late Mycenaean pottery on a number of sites lends colour to the legends of Achaean colonisation there. The memory of two Achaean adventurers – Amphilochus and the indefatigable seer Mopsus – was cherished in some of the names and legends of city foundations; and Mopsus' descendants were still ruling a principality in this region 500 years later, if we may so interpret the mention of the House of Mukshash (or, in Semitic, Bt Mpš) in recently discovered inscriptions at Karatepe. But the culture of these settlements does not seem to have had anything Greek in it in the Dark Age; and though contact with the Aegean was for a short time resumed in the eighth century, the advance of the Assyrian empire under Sargon II and Sennacherib cut short any attempt at Greek colonisation in the Cilician plain.

In the western sector of the coast the great bump of Lycia is a formidable mountain mass rent by precipitous ravines; snowy peaks rise to 10,000 feet, and seem to reach to the zenith when viewed from close inshore. At their foot, where the coast faces east, Dorians of Rhodes planted the colony of Phaselis which played a part in the opening of trade with

Fig. 15. Monumental tomb of Lycian dynast at Xanthus. (Drawing by Scharf.) The shaft is a single block 17 ft high, weighing about 80 tons. The inset marble reliefs (now in the British Museum) are of Greek workmanship in late archaic Aegean style of the beginning of the fifth century. The heroized dead are shown receiving offerings

Egypt; but this was a solitary exception, and in general the Lycians, who seem to have been a people of central Anatolian origin and Indo-European speech, gave a readier welcome to Greek art and architectural forms than to Greek colonists. In the coastal plain of Pamphylia, places like Side, Aspendus and Perge were to rank among the most handsome cities of the Roman world, and Side at least claimed to be an old colony

Fig. 15

Plates 66, 67
68, 69

of Aeolic Cyme. But the search for earlier remains on these sites has so far been unrewarding. Presumably there must have been some Greek settlers on this coast; and the Greek language seems to have been spoken at a number of points, though not always very correctly. But these places, though partly hellenised, do not seem to have ranked as Greek cities in early times; and, conversely, places like Tarsus in the Cilician plain seem to have been cities in early times but they were not Greek.

Cyprus had received waves of Aegean settlers in late Achaean times, and it preserved much of the old Mycenaean way of life with a conservatism that was lacking in Greece itself. But the island was partly Phoenician and a meeting place of two cultures. Under their kings, the cities of Cyprus lived a comfortable life, trading copper and iron to the Levant; and Cypriot vases and Aphrodite figurines of the seventh century are familiar objects to excavators in the southern Aegean lands. But though in early times the Cypriots were advanced in techniques and artistic productivity, they were not subject to the pressures

Fig. 16

Fig. 16. Cypriot terracotta figurine found at Lindos in Rhodes, about 600 BC

that keep creative genius fresh and in the sixth century they began to fall behind in the development of classical Greek civilisation.

In early times the Greeks had little knowledge of the Levant, on whose civilised kingdoms they could make no great impression. Such trade as there was in the Dark Age – or at least before the final stages of that era – probably consisted of occasional visits to the Aegean by the mariners whom Homer knows as Phoenicians, bearing the works of fine craftsmanship that he calls 'Sidonian'. But about the early eighth century the Greeks seem to have sensed commercial possibilities in the Levant. A Greek trading post, perhaps called Posidion (now Al Mina), was set up at the delta of the Orontes; it may not have been the only one on this coast, but it seems to have been at this strategic point above all that the Greeks began to tap the resources of Syria and more distant lands. Ivory and metalwork passed to Greece through the warehouses here; and – what was more significant – Greek art, civilisation and religious ideas were stimulated by the motifs and imagery of an Orient which had itself owed much to the diffusion of Mycenaean culture. It was probably from here also that the Phoenician alphabet first came to Greece. But before this happened some nameless inventors had noted the vowel-sounds suggested by the names of several unwanted letters of the Semitic alphabet and made these letters stand for the vowels themselves; so Greece received and transmitted to her neighbours the first unambiguous phonetic script which (unlike the complicated Bronze Age syllabaries) was not a monopoly of professional scribes but was suitable for common use.

The first Greeks to become known to the kingdoms of the Levant were Ionians; and it has been the fortune of the whole race which we should properly call 'Hellenes' to be known as 'Ionians' (Yavani, Yauna, Yunan) in the East, as well as to pass under the obscure name of 'Greeks' (Graeci) in the West.

But these Ionians in Syria did not come from the Ionia of the Twelve Cities. The origin of the name Yavan may have been in Cyprus; and if we may judge by the pottery they shipped to their new settlement, these newcomers in the East were Ionians of Euboea and the Aegean islands. Ionia itself seems to have had no part in this first commerce and exchange of ideas with the Levant.

The Greek trading colony at Al Mina was by no means an abortive enterprise; and Cypriots and other Greeks traded there in later centuries. But the initial impetus that had carried Greek adventurers and traders to the Levant did not outlast the eighth century. Greek enterprise had perhaps not been confined to peaceful trading. At any rate, when he marched west to reassert Assyrian supremacy on the Levant coast King Sargon had to take active measures against the Greeks. In 712 BC he was at Ashdod, expelling a presumptuous 'Ionian' who had set himself up as despot there. In 709 he was on the shores of Phoenicia 'drawing the Ionians like fish from the sea'; and after this he received the submission of Seven Kings of Ia (perhaps in Cyprus). With the subsequent conquest of Cilicia by Sennacherib and of Egypt by Esarhaddon, these earliest of Greek adventures in the Orient were effectively quenched.

In fact, the occupation of Egypt by the Assyrians was short-lived. Civil war followed the withdrawal of their garrisons, and before the middle of the seventh century Greek raiding-parties were trying their luck in the Delta. This gave the nationalist leader Psammetichus his chance. He was struggling to reunite Egypt; and when bronze-clad Ionian and Carian warriors landed in the Delta he hastened to enlist them in his service. When with their help the Saite kingdom was securely founded, Psammetichus settled these warriors as guards regiments in barracks below Bubastis; and for the next 100 years and more the Pharaohs relied on their Ionic mercenaries. They were not the only rulers to do so; we happen to know that the

EGYPT

brother of the Mytilenaean poet Alcaeus won a sword of honour in the service of Nebuchadnezzar of Babylon. But the Egyptian guard was the most famous. One of its detachments perpetuated its memory by leaving a record of a distant expedition engraved in Greek letters on the legs of the colossi of Rameses II at Abu Simbel, where elephant-hunters and others were to scrawl their names in Ptolemaic times: 'When King Psammetichus went to Elephantine, this text was written by those who sailed with Psammetichus, son of Theocles; they went up beyond Kerkis as far as the river let them go. Potasimto was the commander of the foreigners, and Amasis of the Egyptians. We [i.e. these letters] were engraved by Archon, son of Amoebichus, and Peleqos, son of Eudamus.' Then follow signatures

Fig. 17 of which two are shown on the opposite page. Unfortunately we do not know where Kerkis was, so it is impossible to say how far up the Nile these men from Ionia and Rhodes penetrated – whether just to the second cataract or much higher. But we do know when they went there: Potasimto's coffin has come to light, and it is clear that the expedition took place in the short reign of the younger Psammetichus; its date must be within a year of 591 BC.

Greek traders also were welcomed by the elder Psammetichus. But in the late seventh century they were concentrated in a new treaty port called Naucratis on the Canopic mouth of the Nile. Here merchants from a dozen cities of Ionia and the Aegean lands maintained a self-regulating community, with a common sanctuary where they made dedications to their gods. All Greek trade with Egypt passed through Naucratis; wine and oil no doubt went in, but the principal exchange seems to have been of Egyptian grain against Greek silver.

Trade and mercenary service were the magnets that drew Ionians to Egypt. But there was much for visitors to see and study there. It was no doubt Ionic guardsmen's slang that poked fun at the great tomb monuments by calling them 'buns'

Fig. 17. Signatures of mercenaries of the Ionic Guard at Abu Simbel: 'Pabis of Qolophon, with Psam-matas' (upper), 'Elesibios of Teos' (lower)

(*pyramides*) and gave the granite monoliths the name 'skewers' (*obeliskoi*). But Egypt revealed to the Greeks the potentialities of stone architecture and sculpture. Here, as elsewhere, Greek imagination was kindled by the wonder of the unfamiliar, and in Egypt not least by the immense span of recorded history that was unfolded in front of their eyes. The Greeks were finding their way about the world. But above all it was the Ionians who opened up the new vistas. While they were still politically masters of their own destiny, they had continued Odysseus' quest and 'explored the cities and mentality of many different peoples'. Their horizon by this time extended from the Atlantic coast and Nubia to Babylon and the Russian steppes.

Chapter VI

Architecture and Art in the Ionic Renascence

I**F WE WERE** dependent on archaeology alone we should know very little about the cities of Eastern Greece before the time of the Hellenistic kingdoms; and the little that we can learn about them on the ground would be extremely difficult to interpret. Their situations in the Hellenistic-Roman era are generally known; and most of them still carry some visible traces of the public edifices that were then erected. But remains of previous stages of their existence are elusive. In some places the traces of earlier buildings were swept away in later remodelling or buried under an overlay of heavy foundations and pavements. In other places, as in Chios and Mytilene, ancient strata must lie pinned under the buildings of the modern town. The sites of Myus, Lebedos, Teos, the Lesbian cities, Cyme and Old Cnidus are almost totally unexplored; the early cities of Priene and Erythrae cannot yet be placed with certainty on the map, and the original situations of Colophon, Clazomenae, Ephesus and Halicarnassus are only approximately known. The archaeological evidence for living conditions in early Ionia is consequently exiguous and open to misinterpretation.

EARLY CITIES   At the south end of the island of Chios, where the cultivation of mastic flourishes as it did in antiquity, a forest fire recently revealed the traces of an early Greek settlement, whose ancient name is not known. The site has been cleared by

Fig. 18   British archaeologists. This settlement was built in the seventh century on the western slope of a steep hill which rises above a sheltered harbour. The cottages were built of stone and consisted of a single room, sometimes with a porch at the front. On the hill crest was an altar, which in the sixth century was enclosed in a small stone temple; but by that time the settlement on the slope below seems to have been abandoned.

In addition, there were a couple of old sanctuaries down by the harbour.

This, however, was hardly more than a village, and it sheds no direct light on city life. If only its archaic strata were a little better preserved, Miletus would admirably illustrate the lay-out of a great archaic city; for at points on the site the stratum of destruction of 494 B C has been disengaged. On the peninsula, superimposed upon the traces of Cretan and Mycenaean settle- ment, the German excavators found an old shrine of the city- goddess Athena amid traces of archaic habitation; and there were evidently substantial rooms on the waterfront, though they may have been warehouses rather than dwellings. On the detached citadel hill, half a mile to the south, traces of early houses came to light on a broad shelf. The footings were sub- stantially built of more or less squared masonry and formed

Fig. 18. Site of small town in the south of Chios, looking from the north

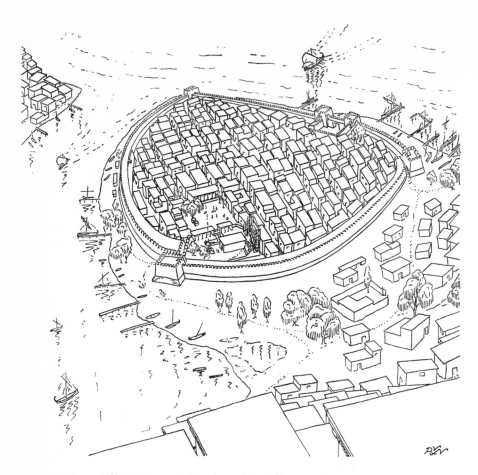

Fig. 19. Old Smyrna as seen from the north in the late seventh century BC. *The new temple is shown as under construction at the near end of the peninsular site. (Drawing by R. V. Nicholls)*

rooms up to 20 feet long; but there does not seem to have been any planned lay-out in this quarter. By 500 BC Miletus may have been a rather old-fashioned town.

The other early town sites tested by excavation are Phocaea and Smyrna. At the former the overlying deposit is deep; and

the Turkish soundings up to the present reveal only the ex⸗
cellent quality of the archaic wall⸗footings. At Smyrna also
the depth of the deposit prevented the excavators from un⸗
covering large areas of the archaic city; but in places the foot⸗
ings of seventh⸗century houses came to light in a stratum of
destruction debris – the city was sacked by the Lydian king
Alyattes about 600 B C. The seventh⸗century city on the penin⸗
sula proves to have been unexpectedly handsome in its build⸗
ings and, apparently also, in its general arrangement. We have
already noted that, on a part of the site at least, some catastrophe
occurred about 700 B C. This seems to have been sufficiently
general to necessitate – or at least permit – a thorough re⸗
modelling of the city in the seventh century. A temple was
constructed on a massive platform at the north end of the site;
new streets were laid out on a north⸗south axis, and houses
were built on a rectangular plan flanking the thoroughfares.
The greater part of the site remains unexcavated, and the draw⸗
ing on the opposite page is of necessity partly conjectural; but it
gives an impression of the seventh⸗century city that is probably
reliable in its main essentials.

Fig. 19

The really significant point here is that the old ground plots
on the peninsular city seem to have been abolished. In antiquity,
as in modern times, the principal impediment to up⸗to⸗date
planning in old⸗established cities was the rights of property⸗
owners; Athens itself, despite the handsome marble buildings
and complexes with which Pericles adorned it, remained to the
end a city of irregular, winding streets. At Smyrna, however, it
seems as though the old irregular plan was completely dis⸗
regarded in the new lay⸗out of the seventh century. The new
town⸗houses were more spacious than their predecessors, and
almost certainly some of the householders were obliged to
move out of the old walled town and live in a suburb on the
adjoining mainland slope. The houses of the seventh century
were well constructed. The walls were of broad flat mud

bricks which rested on finely jointed stone footings three or four feet high, and no doubt the brick was surfaced with fine lime plaster both inside and out. The walls were 18 inches thick, and in many cases there must have been an upper storey. Smyrna had thus abandoned its old village/like lay/out and become an up/to/date city like Miletus – perhaps more so, in/ deed. The roofs were characteristic Mediterranean flat roofs with the surface of loam that needs rolling out after heavy rain. Little attention seems to have been paid to drainage, yet some of the houses had big, comfortable terracotta bath tubs.

In most cases the extent of the individual town/houses at Smyrna could not be ascertained; but on an average they prob/ ably had three rooms on the ground floor. In part of the city – perhaps in the greater part – the houses extended along the sides of the axial streets so as to form a single continuous row separated at the back by a narrow crack from the row that fronted on the next street. The blocks of houses that were thus formed may have been quite long; but the houses on this arrangement seem to have been only one room thick, so the blocks were only 40 feet wide. In all probability one of the rooms in the ground plot of each house was a courtyard, en/ closed by four walls but remaining open to the sky. Besides serving various needs, this will have helped to admit light; and if they were two/storeyed, the houses must have been tolerably spacious. With the incorporation of the courtyard inside the oblong plot and the linking of plots in continuous street/ frontages, we seem to come up against regular town/houses for the first time in the history of Greek architecture.

The old town wall at Smyrna was in disrepair in the seventh century; and if a part of the city population was living in a suburb outside the walls, the incentive to restore the forti/ fication would naturally be lacking. But towards the end of the century, when the menace of Lydia may once again have been felt, a new and stronger wall was built. Nothing now remains

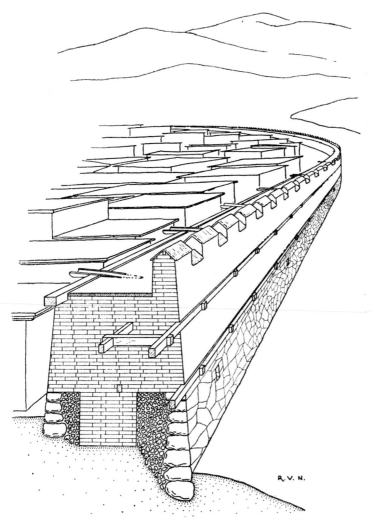

*Fig. 20. City wall at Old Smyrna in the late seventh century BC. (R. V. Nicholls'
restoration)*

Fig. 20 of the superstructure of this wall above the level of the stone base; and the reconstruction shown on the previous page is only intended as one possible interpretation of the archaeo logical evidence. But there is a fair likelihood that timber was used to reinforce the mud brick, and there can be little doubt that the parapet carried battlements. This wall was of great thickness – its base is over 50 feet wide on the east edge of the site, where the foundations of earlier walls have been incorpor ated in it, and the core is firmly packed with mud brick. A fortification like this relied on the sheer strength which rendered it immune to assault by battery or mining; it belonged to the era in military engineering before projecting towers and sally ports were introduced to facilitate a more aggressive type of defence. And in fact this wall presented a serious obstacle to the Lydian king when he came down to the coast and invested Smyrna; it was only surmounted in the end by an enormous siege mound whose rounded crest still rises 70 feet above the flat ground on the north edge of the site. By this means Smyrna was captured. Alyattes the Lydian thereby destroyed a flourish ing and beautiful Greek city. But it was the only success that he achieved against the Ionians in a reign of half a century; for Herodotus tells us that when he advanced from Smyrna to wards Clazomenae he suffered a severe defeat.

SANCTUARIES   There is no sign of a centre of public worship in Dark Age Smyrna; so far as the excavation there permits a judgement, the earliest temple seems to have been of the seventh century. At the renowned sanctuary of Artemis (Diana) at Ephesus the excavations yielded no trace of cult before the early seventh century, and the other temple sites excavated on this coast have yielded nothing as early as this. Such public worship as took place in the Dark Age must in the main have been very simple, and perhaps normally required nothing more than a rough altar for sacrifices. At Miletus the excavators have recently un covered a low oval platform of rough stones which is nearly

7 feet across at its widest. It seems to date to the eighth century
and to have at some time been enclosed in a small precinct. Its
position is under the corner of the classical temple of Athena;
so it is likely that it is in fact an old altar – the oldest yet discovered in Greek Asia Minor. A roofed 'temple' building was
probably not needed there at the time when the altar was laid.
The Greeks performed their public worship in the open air
and did not normally require covered buildings to accom-
modate a congregation. Temples therefore were only built at
the stage when the deity required a house – that is to say, when
there was a sizeable image, together perhaps with gear and
dedications of value, which must stay on the spot and be given
protection. In the eighth century such images may have been
few; and it is perhaps no accident that the earliest Ionic temple
known to us was at a country shrine where one of the most
venerable of Greek idols stood. This was the sanctuary of Hera
on the Ionic island of Samos.

The Samians claimed that their goddess, whom they recognised as the Greek Hera, was born in Samos on the banks of
the stream called Imbrasus; and it was there, at the end of a long
shelving beach three or four miles west of the ancient city, that
their famous sanctuary lay. Apparently there had been a walled
town on this spot in the Late Mycenaean epoch, and the worship of the local goddess may well have been older than the
Dark Age; for under the great altar of the sixth century the
excavators found traces of earlier altars, the rudest of which is
thought to date from the twilight of Mycenaean times. In the
Dark Age there was certainly a rough stone altar there with a
pebbled area facing it; and there may also have been a small
hut of mud brick to house an old wooden idol. The first major
temple, facing east across the pebbled area to the altar, probably
belongs to the eighth century. It had a total width of about
24 English feet, and the roof was supported by a central row of
internal posts. But while the span was limited by the length of

the timbers available to the Samians at the time, there was no corresponding limit set to the length of the building, and the image of the goddess faced up a hall which was a generous 100 feet long. This first temple made way in the seventh century for a successor whose walls rested on footings of ashlar masonry. Some time before this, the original temple had been extended by the addition of an external row of pillars which provided a sort of verandah on at least two of its sides; and this archi-tectural principle, which foreshadows the outer colonnade of Greek 'peripteral' temples, was adopted with wider verandahs in the seventh-century temple also. But the second temple dispensed with the central row of internal pillars and its roof had a clear span of almost 20 feet.

Fig. 21

The construction of this second temple was accompanied by fresh works in the sanctuary area. The much enlarged altar was re-faced in good masonry; the area in front of it seems to have been paved, and the precinct began to be adorned with monu-ments. The most spectacular of these offerings was the huge bronze griffin-head cauldron supported by three twice-life-size kneeling human figures, which (Herodotus tells us) was dedi-cated by the ship-owner Colaeus and his crew as a tithe of their gains on a single voyage – driven by a storm through the Straits of Gibraltar they had been the first of all Greeks to reach the metal market of Tartessus. The position of Colaeus' monu-ment is not known. It may have been in the part of the precinct that lay south of the altar area, because this seems to have been the festal space in which the crowds gathered; but there were monuments in other quarters also, such as the approach on the north-east where the sacred way from the city led to the entrance-pylon. At the south end of the festal area, communi-cating with the sea, there were stone-lined water tanks which may have served for the lustral bath of the goddess. In the late seventh century the western side of the festal area by the stream bank was closed by a long building of the sort that the Greeks

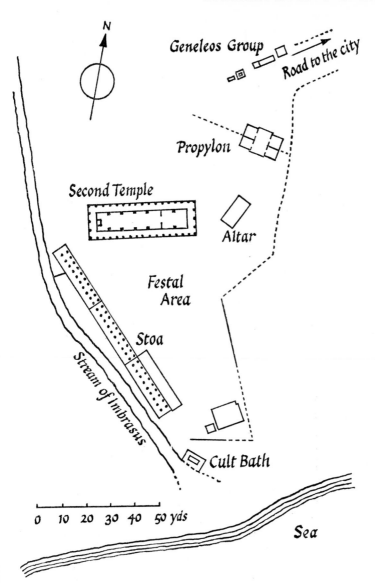

Fig. 21. Plan of Samian Heraeum in the early sixth century BC. *(After Schleif)*

Fig. 22. Bronze cauldron on stand with griffin-heads on the shoulder, found at La Garenne (Loire)

Fig. 23

called 'stoa'. The memory of this word is preserved for us in the epithet 'stoical', which reflects the attitude to life that Zeno first preached in the 'Painted Stoa' at Athens. These stoas were, generally speaking, ornate sheds whose open, colonnaded front faced on to a public place. The Samian stoa here illustrated had a length of 200 Samian feet; its floor was of trodden clay, and the roof was supported by two long rows of pillars or posts, while at the south end a paved promenade ran in front of the pillared walks. This long building will no doubt have been frequented by vendors, entertainers and loiterers, and it could provide a large concourse of pilgrims with shelter against sun or rain.

Magnificent as they must have seemed at the time, these mud/ brick and plaster buildings of the Samian Heraeum were modest by comparison with the gigantic constructions that replaced them in the sixth century. But they serve to show how rapidly the Ionians were progressing in the direction of large/ scale architecture and planning in the seventh century. Stone construction in the Greek architectural orders seems to have been an achievement of the later years of that century. It was to some extent prompted by a growing acquaintance with the grandiose monuments of Egypt. But in this the Greeks were not imitators; they did not copy the forms that they saw in Egypt and the Orient, and in fact the early development of monumental architecture followed different courses on the two opposite sides of the Aegean.

On the Greek mainland the Doric order was quickly established in a canonical form. Above the level of the archi/ trave the detailed construction of the exterior conformed to a set scheme which in its appearance – if not in its precise

Fig. 23. Seventh/century Stoa at the Samian Heraeum. (After the restoration in Athenische Mitteilungen, *vol. 72)*

historical evolution – can fairly be described as 'petrified carpentry'; and the proportions and general design are equally
stereotyped. Though much longer-lived and more widely
known, this Doric architecture is closely akin as an art-form to
Athenian tragedy, which also underwent a gradual development of feeling but admitted no radical change. The early
Doric style of architecture is very much better known than the
Ionic; it can conveniently be set up as a standard in handbooks,
and consequently the characteristic oblong of the ground-plan,
the stepped foundation flush with the outer colonnade and the
tiled roof with its gabled ends have long been regarded as
indispensable features of any respectable Greek temple. But
architecture in the eastern Aegean did not pursue a similar
course. What we know of it points to a variety of treatment
which is in sharp conflict with the rigid conventions of Doric.
We should therefore resist the temptation to explain the early
Ionic style as a slim and sophisticated, somewhat wayward
sister of the masculine Doric. It is true that in the fifth century
the Athenians adapted the Ionic style with taste and subtlety
to serve as an accompaniment and a foil to their native Doric,
and by doing so they set a standard for the international development of the Ionic order; indeed the Ionians themselves accepted

Plate 64

this standard in the fourth century. But it was a peculiar artificial elegance that the Athenians imparted to the Ionic style.
The early architecture of the eastern Aegean seems to have been
altogether freer and less inhibited.

Early temples were simply rooms for the deity, and in the
eastern Aegean they probably comprised for the most part a
single chamber without a porch. Before the enormous temples
of Samos and Ephesus were designed in the second quarter of
the sixth century, the normal width was not more than 20 feet

Fig. 24

unless (as at Neandria in the Troad) the roof had the support
of an inner row of columns. More than anything, the length
of a temple will have depended on the space and funds avail-

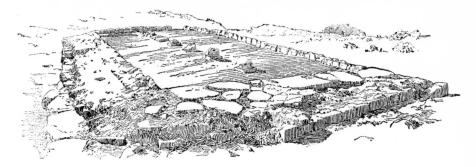

Fig. 24. Temple at Neandria in the Troad, seen from the back, or south-east. (From Koldewey)

able. The original 'hundred-footer' of Samos had a length-breadth proportion of 5 to 1; but the early temple at Smyrna seems to have been squarish in plan, and similar proportions are found in classical Ionic buildings. After thatch was abandoned, roofs may normally have been flat. A level terrace was of course provided for the temple to stand on, and it seems generally to have been revetted with well-jointed masonry on the sides where it rose above the outside ground level. The unfinished temple of the late seventh century in the city at Smyrna offers a good example; but here the high platform had been extended to the south to allow a clear space alongside the temple; and on the edge of this area stood a couple of small stoa-like buildings, between which a pylon at ground level gave access to an inclined processional way. Normally the platform was large enough to allow an open walk round the outside of the temple at the level of the foot of the columns or walls. The earliest stone columns yet known are the drums of soft white tufa which were intended for use in the late seventh-century temple at Smyrna. They were 3 feet in diameter; they were not 'fluted' (vertically channelled) and would perhaps have remained in that condition. In the sixth century the

Plate 9

Fig. 24

number and shape of the flutings on columns varied considerably; 'Aeolic' column-shafts seem normally to have been plain, if not of wood.

Early Ionic architects were evidently more concerned with finding satisfactory solutions to the particular problems that at any given moment confronted them than with establishing fixed conventions like their Doric colleagues; it seems that in Samos, if not also at Ephesus, their rule of proportions was lax enough even in the sixth century to permit them to place an odd number of columns at the back end of the temple despite the fact that there was of course an even number at the front, where entry on the central axis needed to be unobstructed.

If we could see an early Ionic temple still standing in as good condition as some of the early Doric ones in Sicily or southern Italy, we should probably feel that its beauty did not consist so much in the subordination of the different members to a single

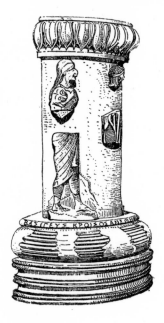

Fig. 25. Sculptured base-drum from the Artemisium at Ephesus, as formerly reconstructed from fragments in the British Museum; the figures are about life-size. (From Durm.) Fragments of lettering on the low foot-roll of some drums indicate that King Croesus was the donor

design as in the intrinsic charm of its decorated parts. At
Ephesus, figured relief sculpture was introduced to distinguish   *Fig. 25*
the bottom drums of some at least of the great columns of the
Artemisium and in a long band which formed a parapet along
the edge of the roof; it may also have been used on other sites
to enliven the edges of temple platforms. In early Ionic architecture, sculpture had no fixed positions above eye-level such as
it had in Doric; and it was mainly by the use of deeply carved
mouldings that the architects sought to break up the sunlight
and give diversity to the stone copings and entablatures. In the
middle quarters of the sixth century Ionic mouldings attained   Plate 11
a voluptuous floridity that can hardly be classed as 'archaic'
any longer. The capitals of the columns exhibit a comparable
development. The massive whitestone piece from the temple at
Smyrna, dating to the late seventh century, shows floral motifs   Plate 13
already well adapted to the different curvatures of the surface;

*Fig. 26. Aeolic capital of the Temple at Neandria,
with volute-piece, roll-member and leaf-crown. (After
Koldewey.) First half of the sixth century* BC.
*Scholars from time to time contest Koldewey's rest-
oration of the capitals with three members and argue
that the pieces come from two distinct series of capitals
(internal and external); but it is unlikely that there was
an external colonnade here*

83

Fig. 26

Plate 12

Fig. 27

Fig. 26

Plate 12

Fig. 26

but the carving itself, originally distinguished by painting in two or three colours, is shallow and timid. A generation or two later, in the Neandria capitals, much greater freedom has been obtained, but with an exuberance that seems almost frivolous. In the 'Ionic' capitals, such as those of the Artemisium at Ephesus, luxuriance and compactness are agreeably harmonised.

We know of three main classes of archaic column-capital in the eastern Aegean. One is the rare 'leaf capital'. This is illustrated – whether rightly restored in two tiers or not – in the drawing of the Treasury that the Phocaeans of Massalia set up at Delphi; if the early piece at Smyrna is to be regarded as a curious variant of it, the Greek leaf capital may have been most at home in northern Ionia. The leaf capital did not quite die out; at any rate it reappears in the Hellenistic architecture of Pergamon. The other two classes are both volute capitals; but they differ greatly from one another in the form of the volute-member and the neck-mouldings. The class with branching spirals, to which the Neandria capitals belong, is commonly called 'Aeolic' because it is in Lesbos and the neighbouring coastlands that such capitals are found; its decoration has some unexplained affinities in the minor arts of the Near East. The third and most enigmatic of all, in which the massive volute member looks as though it were pressed flat like a bolster, is the forerunner of the classical Ionic capital; and it seems that the prestige attaching to the huge temples of Ephesus and Samos had a large part in making this the standard form of eastern Greek capital.

The Neandria capitals had a narrow ledge on top for the beam to rest on; they must have crowned the row of columns inside the temple, and evidently they were intended to carry or prop a line of longitudinal beams running down the central axis of the hall. But as columns assumed their position on the exterior of temples, it became the prime function of volute

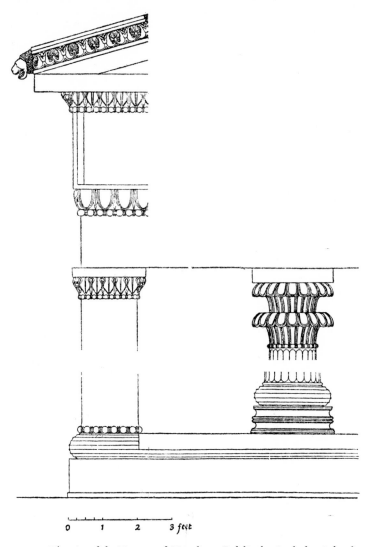

Fig. 27. Elevation of the Treasury of Massalia at Delphi, showing leaf-capital and mouldings. (After Fouilles de Delphes)

capitals to provide an oblong surface for the architrave beams to meet on; and the Ionic capital with its long resting surface was evidently designed for this purpose. As decorative members on the exterior of a building these capitals were admirable. But they had one disadvantage, that their oblong shape gave them short ends and they could not satisfactorily present two adjacent voluted faces so as to turn the corner from the end colonnade to that on a long side. This difficulty was eventually surmounted in Ionic at the cost of making the capitals more nearly square in plan; a prim, elegant form resulted, and the Ionic capital received its place in the universal repertory of architecture. But the 'Aeolic' capital was less tractable, and it does not seem to have outlasted the sixth century.

CRAFTSMAN-
SHIP AND
DEDICATIONS

Fig. 22

Plate 17

Plate 16

In the seventh century fine dedications began to be offered in the sanctuaries of the goddesses. In Samos the bronze workers were pioneers in hollow casting, and among the most frequent dedications in the Heraeum were cauldrons adorned with cast heads of those yawning, peg-topped aristocrats of the mythical menagerie which bear the name of griffins. Ivory carvers seem also to have been at work in Ionia, and figurines and dress pins of ivory, together with inlaid furniture, were evidently valued as costly dedications. So also were fine products of the jeweller's art, though unfortunately these do not often remain for the excavator to find; curiously, the most complete hoard of Ionic craftsmanship of this sort is a treasure which came to light in 1939, buried under the paving of the Sacred Way at Delphi. Amulets and trinkets of Phoenician fayence, possibly made in a factory in Rhodes, were common offerings at temples; among the less common ones are engraved tridacna shells and ostrich eggs imported from the Levant and Egypt. Precious objects of this sort, generally in a fragmentary state, come to light in the waste deposits of sanctuaries. Painted clay vases and terracotta figurines had a wider range of use; and some very fine specimens of such vases have been excavated in houses, where they were evidently used as table or toilet ware. Of the figurines, the best-known series comes from tombs in the island of Rhodes, where flasks in human or animal form were manufactured as containers for scented oil; some of these are so Ionic in style and so exquisite in their finish that one is tempted to suppose that the workshops in Rhodes were origin~ally set up by Ionians.

Plates 14, 15

The emancipation of art from the austere linear conventions of the Geometric style came late in eastern Greece. In vase painting it was not until the middle of the seventh century that freehand drawing became the fashion; and the 'orientalising' style, which prevailed there during the next hundred years, aimed at providing pleasing decorative designs rather than major paintings in miniature. East Greek vase painting is thus less serious in its artistic ambitions than the leading schools of

Fig. 28. Animals on East Greek orientalizing vases (After Kinch)

mainland Greece, though from time to time it drew inspiration from mainland styles and techniques. Its repertory of animal and vegetable forms is a small one; and the ornament generally runs in continuous bands on which a single scheme is repeated indefinitely; the basic patterns are running lotus scrolls and files of walking or grazing goats, always of course seen in profile view. Though now and again a handsome new motif was invented – witness the seated griffins or waddling geese – the pictorial art remained subordinate to the overall scheme governing the decoration. Human figures hardly ever appear; and when they do, they are usually inept.

Plate 16

Fig. 28

CHAPTER VII

Cities and Individuals in the Ionic Renascence

BY THE SIXTH CENTURY the cities of the Eastern Greeks had long since made good in their struggle for existence, and each of the leading ones had developed its own peculiar character. To the Lesbians at least, political power was worth struggling for; otherwise, what sounds through the surviving poems of the time is fierce enjoyment of the moment and the wistful backward glance. In the Dorian South nothing much was afoot. The people of Cos were content with their fertile fields, and, except perhaps for Lindos, the cities of Rhodes made no great use of their position on the highway of commerce. Their neighbours of Cnidus were a more vigorous, forthright people; having too little arable land at the foot of their sierras, they seem to have annexed the neighbouring valleys, and they sent out emigrants to live a piratical, communistic life in the Lipari islands; but in general the southern Dorians had not yet sniffed the wind of change and progress.

In Ionia the differences between the individual cities were most marked. Historically, such differences are important; for they will to some extent have prompted healthy rivalry between cities, and they prevented Greek civilisation from becoming uniform and hidebound. The seafaring Phocaeans had developed the uncompromising toughness that colours their subsequent activities: they long maintained this character, for Livy tells us of their quixotic gallantry in the cause of Antiochus the Great when the Roman commander assaulted Phocaea in 190 BC; the warlike Romans were so severely handled that the praetor had to call for a parley and beg the Phocaeans not to take the war so seriously. Fretted by the incessant gales from the mouth of the gulf, the people of Clazomenae grew up rest-less and volatile. On the other side of the headland, Teos slumbered in its hollow, taking life as it came and unwilling ever to struggle; the Teians opened their gates to all assailants, and their saddest hour came when, rather than defend them-selves, they handed over to the same Roman praetor all the wine that they were waiting to sell to Antiochus. The people of Chios made their fortune in finance, wine and the slave trade; and their public policy was governed by cautious con-siderations of prudence and self-interest. The prosperity of Colophon depended on control of the inland plain, and a decline seems to have started as early as the sixth century when the Lydians gained possession there. Colophon and Smyrna held on longest to the tradition of epic poetry. Ephesus also had close connections with the Lydians and played little part in Greek affairs. The little country town of Priene by the Maeander mouth suffered grievously under the Lydians and Persians; later, it produced the leading authorities on agriculture, and, with true farmers' cunning, the Prienians gained a reputa-tion as the experts in boundary litigation.

The most remarkable contrast is that between Miletus and its great neighbour, the island of Samos. Hostility was normal between them; for Samos lay upwind off Miletus and could interfere with her rival's commerce. Samos controlled the one relatively safe crossing of the Aegean for warships. Her craft no doubt had saucy lines like those of Samian caïques in modern times and were fast enough to nip across the straits before a gale could get up. The ancient Samians were addicted to piracy and raiding; and though the island was left desolate in the Middle Ages and re-peopled with new settlers from Lesbos, geographical circumstance has made these modern Samians true successors of the ancient ones. As recently as 1949 they were raiding the Turkish coast. In the sixth century BC Samos ruled the seas for a time, and again in the fifth its navy was the one serious rival to Athens. The Samians were great opportunists, and at the same time they were never so resolute as when they were defending a lost cause. The Milesians, by contrast, seem generally to have been steady, austere and honourable in their transactions. In the sixth century Miletus was the home of rational thought, and – if one may speak in such terms – the first university of Greece. The Milesians were the greatest pure scientists, while the Samians excelled in bold engineering, experiment and the practical applications of science; it was, no doubt, for experiments in breeding that Polycrates of Samos imported the thoroughbred Milesian sheep, whose wool was the finest in the Greek world.

In Homer's age, specialists had little place; the singer, who was the most skilled of craftsmen, was very much a man of the world; and the quality which was most admired was all-round ability. We know little about thought in the seventh century; but when we reach the first thinkers to become public cele- brities in Greece – the Seven Sages, who lived about the be- ginning of the sixth century – we cannot help observing, as Cicero did and Plato was at pains to deny, that they were also men of affairs with a wide range of attainments. There was constant dispute in ancient Greece about the tally of the Seven; but a majority of Eastern Greeks was always accepted in the canon, and it was universally agreed that the greatest of them all was Thales the Milesian. In the views attributed to Thales by later writers we are conscious for the first time of a brain that is free from preconceived notions about man's origin and the universe; he judged by the light of reason and was capable of constructing theories that could be critically examined. People therefore talk as though Thales were the inventor of rational thought; but this probably does less than justice to his anony- mous predecessors. The acknowledged pre-eminence of Thales and his fellow Sages is not unconnected with the new sense of Hellenic unity that was gripping the Aegean world; prior

EARLY
THINKERS

to this, only poetry could circulate and leave its mark, but in the generation of the Sages new ideas were becoming matters of public interest.

Thales' reputation in the ancient world rested above all on achievements which had a practical value or were potentially useful. He made advances in surveying and geometry – for example, he reckoned the height of the Pyramids from their shadow; and he worked out a method of calculating the distance of ships at sea. He also helped navigators by defining the celestial pole more precisely; and taking what in effect was a bold chance – for it might have happened in the night-time – he astonished the Greek world by successfully predicting an eclipse of the sun (probably that of May 585 BC). He is said to have diverted the river Halys to allow Croesus' army to cross, and also to have made a fortune by foreseeing a good year for olives and renting the oil presses in advance.

Thales maintained that the earth floats on water. This may not in itself be any great advance on Homer's allegorical notion of Ocean as the genesis of all things. But in another direction it represents an advance, because Thales' concern was with the physical problem of matter in the universe, and his contention was that water is the primary substance from which other things are formed. Thales is the first known personage in the line of Ionic, and more particularly, Milesian, physicists who explored the material world and tried to offer explanations to fit the observed facts. These men lacked optical instruments and apparatus for measuring distance and time; but they examined nature (*physis*) in many of her aspects, and they studied beaches and clay deposits, evaporation and condensation, winds, temperature, phosphorescence, magnetism and the technical processes used in everyday life.

It may be that Thales was the greatest single figure in the evolution of Greek rational thought. But as a scientist he seems to have been eclipsed by his own pupil and fellow-Milesian,

Anaximander. We know some of the conclusions that Anaximander reached, but unfortunately we are not told by what steps he reached them. His mental attitude is revealed by a curious little story told about him: one day, when Anaximander was singing, his attention was drawn to the fact that the children were laughing at him; instead of being angry, he remarked, 'In that case I must try to sing better for their sake.' He too was a practical man, for he was chosen to lead a colony to the North-east; and he made a map of the earth and constructed sun-clocks.

In Anaximander's view the original substance was not one of the recognised elements, but was a neutral matter, described as the 'Infinite (or Unlimited)', out of which the elements were formed. This seems a very bold idea; but in postulating a substance whose existence could not be tested by the human senses he may have been influenced by the study of wind, which is a powerful invisible force or substance. From the 'Infinite' all the heavens and the worlds contained in them were separated off, and to it they must necessarily return; and propulsion was evidently inherent in this original substance. Anaximander's system was a comprehensive one. It explained the generation of the heavens with their fiery concentrations and the earth as a disk poised in the centre. He reckoned that the seas are diminishing and the earth is drying out – a conclusion that was presumably based on the presence of marine shells on land high above sea-level. If his worlds were not contemporary but successive ones, maybe he considered that only a theory of previous cycles could somehow explain evidence of the land having once been more advanced than it is now. Some of his cosmology may seem to us cumbrous, or even crude. But it was revolutionary thinking in its time. So too, in the biological field, was his deduction that since man passes through a long period of helplessness after birth, the original human beings could not have survived without some special protection. The emancipation of Ionic thought was complete when Anaxi-mander conceived the idea that the first form of life consisted of creatures with a thorny bark which were generated in warm slime and that it was from their successors on dry land that man was first hatched. The highest level of Ionic abstract reasoning was reached when he argued that the earth does not require any support underneath: being equidistant from the extremities of the universe, it must be equally inclined to move in every direction; and since it cannot move simultaneously in opposite directions, it must necessarily stay where it is.

The great man's successors lacked his boldness. They thought that the earth-disk must be thin like a leaf and so able to ride on air (Plato later ridiculed them for stuffing air under the earth like a base under a kneading-trough, and so created the absurd notion of a hovercraft-contraption suspended over a void). The next generation did make some improvements in Anaximander's general system; and his theory that life origi-nated in the primeval mud was advanced by close observation of shells and marine fossils on land. But after Anaximander the study of physics was never again quite such an adventure. His immediate follower at Miletus, Anaximenes, seems by com-parison to be like a conventional scholar succeeding to an existing professorship; and elsewhere thought was turning for the time being in other directions.

ECONOMIC
AND
POLITICAL
GROWTH

Fig. 29

With the growth of Black Sea trade, the Ionic cities were able to rely on imported grain and so to turn more to specialised production and industry. Money, in the form of coins whose value was officially certified by the stamp of an issuing author-ity, was probably a Lydian invention; and it may at first have been intended as a convenience for the payment of troops. But in the sixth century many Greek cities were issuing their own coins, and commercial transactions were thus greatly facilitated. Although land may have been regarded as the soundest invest-ment, there was no feeling yet that trade was an ungentlemanly activity; and the poetess Sappho's brother seems to have done business in Egypt. Miletus and Teos became famous for their wool, and in the fifth century Miletus also had the leading furniture industry. A merchant of Chios supplied eunuchs to Ephesus and the Persians. Silks were exported from Cos; wines of different characters came from Chios and Mytilene, and later from the South Dorian cities. We learn from the ancient writers that Caria was famous for its honey, Rhodes for its sponges, Erythrae and the island of Nisyros for mill stones, Colophon for resin, Chios for mastic gum, Myus for its fisheries, Cnidus for herbs, Caunus for figs, Cos for raisins, Aegae for saffron; and we hear of local specialities, like the prawns of Smyrna or the red mullet of Teichiussa. As regards imports, grain came from Egypt as well as from the Scythians, salt fish, steel and red ochre from the Black Sea, silver and wine came to Chios from the coast of Thrace, metals to Phocaea from Tartessus, copper was perhaps brought to Samos from Cyprus; Sardis, the Lydian capital, was the source of pale gold, unguent and leatherwork; and, in the Aegean, Athens exported oil, Corinth scent and fine pottery; broadswords of Chalcis in Euboea were admired in Mytilene, and the best marble was brought from the islands of Naxos and Paros.

Fig. 29. Royal Lydian gold stater, type of Croesus' reign (about 561–547)

After hereditary monarchy came to an end in Ionia, families of royal descent seem to have enjoyed special privileges in two or three places, but in general the cities must have been self-governing communities of citizens who may for the most part have been fairly well-to-do. With the Lydian wars, however, there may have been increasing poverty in some of the cities; and it is certain that by the fifth century, when Ionic trade was much reduced, a fairly clear distinction had come to exist between the many and the landowning few. Tyrants or political bosses arose in a number of places during the sixth century; and some of them, like Polycrates at Samos, made their cities stronger and more flourishing than before. It is sometimes claimed that these tyrants gained power by championing the people against oppression by the few. But Aristotle expressly tells us that in Ionia this was not the case; the tyrants there won their position by continuing to hold public office. At Miletus the background of the tyranny may have been continual strife between the farmers and the mercantile class. In Chios also there may have been political trouble in the first half of the sixth century; for we have a mutilated inscription in which the judicial duties of the magistrates and the people's council were openly set out for everyone to read, and it is generally assumed that (though found in the countryside) this was an ordinance of the sovereign city on the island and not just a minor reform in one of the villages.

The reader may be disappointed at the lack of crispness in this very brief sketch of early Ionic political development; for modern scholars are agreed that in the states of the Greek mainland there was a general progression from Dark Age kingship to the rule of the 'best' and government by the wealthy 'few', and a parallel development has been postulated for Ionia. But, slight though it is, the evidence for seventh-century Ionia does not support this view; and we do not seem justified in supposing that there existed 'masses' of poor citizens so long as sufficient land was available. The social inequality of the fifth century, when strife flared up between the many and the land-owning few in some of the Ionic cities under Athenian rule, may have resulted in the main from the Lydian and Persian conquest.

In Mytilene, where probably there was not much urban population, the families may have counted for more. Aristotle tells us a little of what was happening there in the early sixth century; and snatches of lyrics of the hard-drinking poet Alcaeus help to fill out the account. In the seventh century there was the normal system of council and popular assembly. But about 600 BC an old family attempted to wield power by violent means; and after its fall, rival family groups contended for domination until Pittacus was elected absolute ruler for a period of ten years. Pittacus did not change the constitution, which in itself was no doubt broadly enough based; but he did introduce new laws which were painted up on wood, and he doubled the penalties for offences committed in drunkenness. Alcaeus railed against Pittacus and complained bitterly of the tempest in which his 'ship' was wallowing. In one of his poems he says that he is keeping his feet out of harm's way, sitting where the Lesbian maidens come to be judged in their annual beauty competition; but on other occasions he reveals that he was implicated in attempts to seize power, once with Lydian gold to back him. Pittacus completed his ten-year task. He succeeded in setting Mytilene on an even keel, and he was magnanimous enough to let the poet go unpunished when finally he caught him. The judgement of posterity was in favour of Pittacus; for with one accord the Greeks named him among the Seven Sages.

CHAPTER VIII

The Climax of Eastern Greek
Achievement

THE PERSIAN
CONQUEST IN THE FIRST HALF of the sixth century Ionic civilisation
matured; in life and thought, as in the architectural carvings,
the sharp edges had been rounded off, and men and women
had acquired poise and a well-plenished graciousness by the
time that Croesus made himself master of the Greek sea-board.
Croesus had come to the throne of Lydia about 561 BC. He
quickly reduced the Greek cities of the coast except for Miletus.
But, with his admiration for Greek culture, he proved a
generous conqueror; and in fact later generations of Greeks
cultivated his memory with an affectionate regard as though he
had been one of themselves. He had barely reigned 14 years
when he rode east across the Halys to challenge Cyrus the
Persian. After an indecisive campaign he returned home and
dismissed his levies for the winter. But Cyrus unexpectedly
followed him up, won a decisive victory in the Lydian plain,
and – thanks to his mountaineers who scaled the undefended

Plate 7 cliff – stormed the citadel of Sardis before Croesus' reinforce-
ments could arrive. The battle in the plain below Sardis, in
which no Greek state had a part, is the first important battle in
Greek history. Curiously, it foreshadows the subsequent en-
counters between Greeks and Persians. A corps of the Ionic
foot-guards had been sent by Pharaoh Amasis to assist Croesus
against the common enemy. The Lydian cavalry were soon
driven off the field, because, Herodotus says, their horses could
not stand the sight or smell of the camels that had been cun-
ningly stationed in the Persian van. But the foot-guards continued to press onward in their phalanx; and like the Ten
Thousand at Cunaxa in 401 BC they would not relinquish

their possession of the field until the victor offered them a treaty. The invincibility of Greek infantry was thus revealed before Greeks and Persians ever went to war with one another.

Cyrus was an Achaemenid by birth and had succeeded to a vassal-kingdom in the Persian highlands. But some years previous to the Lydian war he had exploited the dynastic feuds to which he was heir, and by overthrowing Astyages the Mede he had given the Persians mastery over the Median empire. Now, after overthrowing Croesus, he proceeded to annex the Lydian empire by right of conquest. When he set off for home, he left a Lydian called Pactyes in charge of the treasure at Sardis. But Pactyes broke out in revolt, and absconding with the royal treasure he took refuge in the Greek city of Cyme. The Persian demanded his return, and the people of Cyme were torn between the conflicting demands of moral duty and expediency: the man was a suppliant and entitled to protection, but Cyrus' attitude towards the Greek cities would depend on their action in this crisis.

Fig. 30. Persian guardsman in battle-dress, from a relief of Persepolis

The story of Pactyes is a historical turning-point and Herodotus relates it at length. But, in the twist he gives to it, it also serves to illustrate the flaw in Ionic character. The people of Cyme sent to the great Milesian oracle at Didyma to ask the god's advice. Miletus of course had everything to lose by offending the conqueror of Croesus; and Apollo of Didyma answered that Pactyes should be surrendered. Now, among the Cymaeans opposed to this course was a man called Aristodicus. He went in person to confront the oracle and received the same reply as before. He then walked round the court pulling the young sparrows out of their nests, until the god's voice rang out from the shrine reviling him and asking, 'How dare you harry my suppliants?' And Aristodicus called back, 'But, Master, are you not bidding us betray our suppliant?' This could not have happened in Old Greece, where (as Heraclitus says) 'the Lord, whose oracle is at Delphi, neither declares nor conceals – he gives a sign.' But the Ionic god could not bear to lose an argument – rather than that, he would reverse the fate of Ionia. 'Yes,' he cried, 'that is my bidding, to bring you to a bad end for approaching my oracle with talk of betraying suppliants.' So the Cymaeans refused Cyrus' demand and shipped Pactyes across the water. But prudent citizens of Chios dragged him from the altar and handed him over to the Persians in exchange for the territory they owned on the main-land of Asia Minor.

After the revolt of Pactyes, Lydia was demilitarised; and instead of being the metropolis of the Greek East, Sardis be-came capital of the Persian West. Harpagus, the right-hand man of Cyrus, promptly came down to the coast with the Persian siege train and assaulted the cities. In the far south he met with prolonged resistance; and Miletus was inaccessible enough to preserve its independence; but one by one the other coastal cities were captured. The Phocaeans boarded their war-ships, and a large part of them sailed west to Corsica – in the next chapter we shall come across descendants of theirs at Elea on the Italian coast; and a body of the inhabitants of Teos crossed to Thrace and founded Abdera, the home of brilliant thinkers in the fifth century. The colonies in northern Asia Minor also surrendered; and thus the Greeks of the East were all subjected to Persian rule. In early days at least, this rule was probably easy-going, and the Persians were tolerant in matters of religion and local customs. But the loss of freedom seems to have brought with it a certain loss of self-reliance and enter-prise; and of course many adventurous Ionians had taken the opportunity to emigrate. After this time, most of the great Ionic achievements occurred in Italy, in Athens, in Thrace, or in the Orient.

THE GREAT
TEMPLES

For a generation or so Miletus and the great island-cities pre-served their freedom, and consequently we do not at first perceive a decline in creative impulses in Ionia. The climax of monumentality, in fact, had just been reached in the time of Croesus. With their talent for applied science, the Samians had conceived the notion of building a new temple to their goddess on a scale never before envisaged in the Greek world. Their engineer Theodorus prepared the ground by diverting the river Imbrasus a hundred yards to the west; and a low platform was laid out, 350 feet long and about half as wide. On this foundation an enormous limestone temple was erected. Its columns were $4\frac{1}{2}$ feet in diameter and must have stood nearly 40 feet high; the shafts were not set direct on the pavement but rested on massive moulded bases. There is so little surviving of the superstructure that one is almost tempted to doubt whether the building ever rose above the level of the column drums; but a stratum of broken roof tiles was found in the excavation, so part of the temple seems to have been covered over. This building was commonly known as the 'Labyrinth'. The same engineer is named also as consultant at Ephesus, where a grand new temple of Artemis was planned on the alluvium of the Cayster mouth. Croesus himself seems to have been favourably disposed towards Ephesus; and he made generous subsidies to this new temple, which was being erected about 550 BC.

Fig. 25

Both the Samian Labyrinth and the Artemisium of Ephesus were colossal undertakings. It is perhaps a little difficult to believe that these buildings were designed with fullscale gabled roofs. But even if the central nave of the shrines was partly open to the sky – and this is far from certain – the outer part of the structure was in either case so immense as to require over 100 great columns arranged in a double row all round the building. The entablature that rested on the columns was shallow and light in comparison with the Doric order. The columns were consequently slender in proportion to their height and must have given the impression of soaring upward into the sky. The contrast between the Ionic order here and the contemporary Doric of the Greek mainland may not have been entirely unlike that of our own Perpendicular and Norman. The Doric in fact was seen at its best with its squat mass defying the elements on a citadel rock, whereas the Ionic preferred to aspire heavenward from the flat ground.

In the rivalry that prompted these gigantic buildings, the Ephesians were concerned to outdo the Samians. Not only did they borrow their engineer, but they laid out the Artemisium on an even grander scale than the Labyrinth. The Artemisium, with its lavish use of marble and sculptured decoration, was altogether the more extravagant of the two undertakings. Frag[>] ments of its capitals and mouldings are preserved, and they mark the climax of Ionic floridity. As we have seen, some of the columns rested on sculptured pedestals; and a sculptured marble frieze ran as a parapet along the edge of the roof. The Artemisium benefited from the generous aid of King Croesus; but it was not finished at the time of the Persian conquest, and it is not in fact certain that it had been completed before it was set on fire in 356 BC by a man called Herostratus who was determined to immortalise himself. The temple of Samian Hera was burned down in the sixth century, possibly at the time when the Persians devastated the island soon after 520 BC; it was replaced by a design which was even more ambitious and actually larger than the Artemisium of Ephesus, but this second Labyrinth never reached completion. In the later sixth century, Chios and Miletus also built themselves handsome temples – the latter at Didyma; and apparently a temple with an 'Aeolic' outer colonnade was built in the middle of the island of Lesbos. Of the temple at Didyma too little is known; the others were not on so huge a scale as the giant temples of Samos and Ephesus, and here again very little survives. Small temples of simpler construction were probably numerous on the coast in the later sixth century, to judge by the fragments of terracotta reliefs and ornamental tile[>]ends that have come to light in different places.

Plate 12

The great sanctuaries of Ionia, together with the broad avenues that led up to them, must have glittered with marble dedications in the mid sixth century. The early Ionians had most naturally expressed themselves in music and language. They had not looked to art as a medium for portraying narrative and legend; and probably they did not themselves conceive the idea of setting up marble statues as perpetual memorials of individual munificence or civic and family pride. Though they had become familiar with the great stone effigies of the Egyptian kings, it is doubtful whether they would have turned to monumental sculpture if the brilliant success of the new art of marble carving in the central Aegean islands had not inspired them to emulation. The Ionians were thus slow in turning to sculpture; but when the Southern Ionic cities applied their ingenuity to this art in the early sixth century they succeeded in creating a distinctive sculptural style of their own.

The island of Naxos in the central Aegean was the home of the first Greek school of marble carving in the seventh century. At the beginning of the sixth century the Samians seem to have made common cause with the masons of Naxos; for at that time there appears to have been much resemblance in the marble carving of the two centres, and Naxos apparently shared in the creation of the Ionic capital with its bolsterlike volutemember. In one respect, however, the Samian sculptural style seems to have differed at the outset; it avoided the angular severity of the Naxian. Among the earliest of the great marble dedications of the Samian Heraeum was a row of statues that were set up on a long dais opposite the entrance to the sanctuary. It represents a family of six, including a woman reclining as though at a banquet – she is the dedicator and may perhaps be grandmother, a seated lady called Phileia, and the daughters, of whom one (named Philippa) is preserved; the whole group bore the legend 'Geneleos made us'. The master Geneleos was not so famous as to receive mention from ancient

Fig. 21
Fig. 31

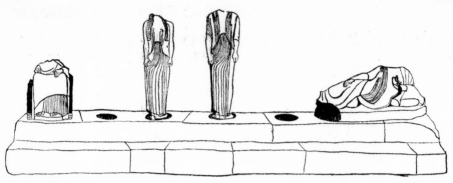

Fig. 31. The Geneleos Group as reassembled in Samos by the German excavators; Philippa was almost 6 ft high. About 570 BC

Plates 18, 19

art-historians. More famous, perhaps, was his contemporary who carved the statue known as the 'Hera' of Cheramyes, now in the Louvre; for, in any age, this dedication would stand out as a remarkable creation. Its form at first sight resembles a tree-trunk, and scholars used to regard it as a primitive adaptation of the forms of wood-carving. In fact, if we needed to find an ancestry for the cylindrical form, we should do better to derive it from wheel-made terracotta images. But this gracious lady with her offering stands in her own right as an artistic concep-tion worth our consideration.

This statue that Cheramyes dedicated proves on closer inspection to be highly sophisticated. The lady gains height, and therewith stateliness, from an excessive length of leg which is concealed by her cylindrical skirt – we realise this if we stop to consider where her knees should come. To achieve this effect, the crinkly skirt, which forms the lower part of the dress, rigidly encases the figure. By way of contrast, a woolly mantle, with heavier diagonal folds, emphasises the softness of the breast and creates an arc of shadow over the swelling of the stomach. The head, which unfortunately is lost, must have been well rounded in form and fitted snugly on the shoulders. Nevertheless, if we imagine it in position, the figure might have seemed to be too sharply divided into different parts, each having its own particular form and texture. The sculptor has wanted to stress the unity of what in the marble is one; he has therefore enveloped a large part of the figure in a smooth shawl which passed over the lady's head and hangs down her back to ankle-level; this garment was evidently intended to unite the rounded head with the cylindrical skirt, and its long ribbon-like seams emphasise the gently curving vertical lines. Seams and contrasted materials will have been distinguished by colour – these statues were of course delicately painted. The features, though they will hardly have been so piquant as those of the veiled lady from Miletus, would have drawn attention upward from the trunk. Finally, there are many little subtleties and quaint touches that catch the spectator's eye and keep him from becoming bored; and the statue has the rare virtue of being worth looking at from every angle. All in all, this was a lady of rank and fashion; and her creator must have been an artist of keen sensibility.

Plate 22

Our knowledge of these early sculptures of Southern Ionia comes mainly from Samos and Milesian Didyma. We find in them a considerable variety of schemes. In mainland Greece, early male statues were by convention standing youths in spare, athletic nudity. In Ionia such figures do sometimes occur. But at the same time it was not unbecoming for a man to be clothed or undignified for him to sit down; and a portly figure was the mark of one who could afford to eat well – after all, only a pauper or a fool remains thin. The standing Samian gentleman shown here and the seated potentates of Didyma are examples of full-grown Ionic manhood. Unfortunately, very few of these sculptures have remained unspoiled by weathering. But the general conception of sculptural form is plainly visible. The South Ionic sculptors, like their friends the physicists, seem to have been concerned with problems of abstract form; the sphere, the cylinder and the cube generally provide the basic

Plates 20, 21

Plate 24

Plate 23
Plate 25

structure; and in the treatment of surfaces we are at times astonished by the economy with which the artist has attained his ends – so sparingly are decorative patterns used to offset the great expanses of unadorned plainness. The captive lion of the Berlin Museum, looking past the visitor with eyes in which hope has died, shows how delusively simple sculptural planes can be. Two Milesian heads demonstrate with how little apparent effort femininity can be rendered: in the one case, the subtle, veiled mysteriousness of a shy young woman, in the other – we may imagine – the more complacent charm of a temple courtesan. Some of the seated figures also show a grow‑ing interest in the recognition of substances; the soft flesh is subtly distinguished from the hard throne, yet in the over‑all design the two remain one and indivisible.

In Samos after the middle of the sixth century the develop‑ment of hollow‑casting gave birth to a new art, life‑size bronze sculpture; but, unfortunately, nothing of this has survived. At the same time, Samian marble carving seems to show a peculiar relationship between artistic design and mechanical processes; this is already to be seen in the horizontal mouldings of the lathe‑turned column bases of the Labyrinth, and a similar harmony distinguishes the carved palmette‑crowns of marble gravestones found in the island.

Ephesus had its sculptor's yards while the Artemisium was being built, and there was beautiful carving both on the column bases there and on similar sculptures found at Sardis; but artists may have gathered from the islands, and we can‑not recognise an Ephesian style with certainty. Chios may have been early in the field, and it was certainly the home of famous sculptors in the sixth century. One of them, Archermus by name, made a figure of Victory that has been dug up in Delos; in this well‑known statue the goddess is shown winged, and poised on her pedestal as though she were ploughing her way through the air. This is a fashionable, extroverted art. The sculptors of Chios were also among those who experimented with an artistic scheme that was to become the standard of Aegean fashion in the later sixth century – the well-dressed lady in a voluminous, semi-transparent linen dress, with a curiously complicated mantle worn over one shoulder. It is not clear where and how this sculptural scheme originated; but in its fully developed form it is familiar as the mode of the archaic Maidens of the Athenian Acropolis; and, among the ones found there, those that are thought to be the work of Chian sculptors are especially distinguished by their finesse and elaborate coiffures. In contrast to South Ionic abstraction, this dazzling artistry has a more worldly appeal, as though its patrons counted every curl to make sure they had got their money's worth.

Plate 22

New developments occurred in painting also in mid sixth-century Ionia. Before this time the vase-painters of Corinth and

EAST GREEK
PAINTING

Fig. 32. 'Fikellura' amphora, found in a tomb in Rhodes, now in the British Museum; partridge. Ht 12 in., mid sixth century BC

Athens had devised a pictorial technique in which the dark silhouettes were articulated by fine engraved detail and human figures were convincingly deployed in movement and action; in this way they had developed a narrative style with a future. This Black Figure technique was brought to a singular perfection by Athenian vase-painters; and when it approached its peak in the second quarter of the sixth century, the influence of this sensitive medium began to make itself felt in Ionia. In the south, in Samos, Miletus and Rhodes, a compromise was reached between the old and new styles. The old Ionic idea of a harmonious relationship between vase-form and decoration was not abandoned; and the new manner of silhouette-drawing and narrative was tempered by a peculiar formality. The resulting style of drawing is broad, simple and effective; vases decorated in this style are very distinctive, and have received the generic name 'Fikellura' from the cemetery in Rhodes where specimens of the class were once discovered.

Fig. 32
Plate 26

In Northern Ionia the influence of Athenian painting was much more directly felt, and a number of different workshops began to produce Black Figure vases. Only Chios stood apart, unwilling to abandon its porcelain-like sphinx-pattern ware. The new Black Figure workshops were mostly short-lived, and some classes of vases reflect the creative genius of individuals rather than schools. In one case it seems possible to trace the career of a North Ionic painter, first at home, and then in central Italy, to which presumably he emigrated at the time of the Persian conquest. This exodus in fact split Ionic painting in two. In the East there developed a fairly uniform style – that commonly called 'Clazomenian' – which is known from discoveries in Northern Ionia, at the Greek settlements in Egypt, and to a lesser degree in the Black Sea colonies; in Italy several schools of painting emerged which seem, initially at least, to have had a distinctively Ionic character.

Plate 27

The western schools of 'Ionic' painting have a touch of

gaiety, and at their best they can be both interesting and imaginative. The painters reacted to the Italian background of their
new lives, and some of the workshops seem gradually to have
passed into Etruscan hands. A refreshing element in this art is
the interest in landscape. Ionic influence seems also to be
recognisable in wall-paintings of some Etruscan chamber
tombs. One of the most talented of these western painters was the
'Caeretan' master, who set up in business with a colleague in
the South Etruscan city of Caere; he specialised in painting
dumpy water-jars and had a genius for depicting themes of the
Greek mythology in a humorous, earthbound style.

Plates 29, 30,
31

The 'Clazomenian' style in the East was also capable of gay
touches, and some of the schemes are attractive. The painters
could not equal the finest Athenian draughtsmanship of their
time. But they did, nevertheless, evolve a larger pictorial style.
Up to the present, no wall-paintings have come to light in
Ionia itself; but fragments of plaster found in buildings of the
early Persian period at Gordion come from murals done in a
North Ionic style. Battle-scenes and heraldically grouped animals decorate the 'Clazomenian' terracotta coffins (*sarcophagi*)

Plate 28

*Fig. 33. Mixed battle scenes painted on lid of a 'Clazomenian' sarcophagus in the British Museum. About
525 BC*

of the later sixth and early fifth century, of which many dozens
have been unearthed in the North Ionic region; and at times
the painters betray a knowledge of the latest advances in
Athenian painting. Finally, excavations have brought to light

Fig. 33, Plates 32,
33

Fig. 34

many fragments of terracotta friezes which formed parapets and ornamental revetments of palace and temple roofs in Northern Ionia and the Aeolis; they are executed in painted relief in a florid style which has much in common with the terracotta sarcophagi. The favourite themes are chariot scenes and banquets. The drawing on this page shows such a scene, reconstructed from fragments discovered in the excavation of one of the Aeolic towns where Cyrus settled the mercenaries of the Egyptian guard after the fall of Sardis. In works such as we have been viewing, Ionic painting reached its maturity within the conventions of an archaic art. But it had no immediate future.

Fig. 34. Terracotta relief panel, from Swedish-German excavations at Buruncuk in the Hermus Plain. North Ionic work of about 525 BC. (After Kjellberg)

CHAPTER IX

The Era of Dominant Personalities

IN PRECEDING CHAPTERS we have come across Pho⁄
caean ships sailing to the West, and North Ionic artists
settling in central Italy. There may also have been some influ⁄
ence from Ionia on western architecture and in other spheres of
human industry; but for the most part such impulses are not
easy to estimate. The one undeniable and profound transforma⁄
tion that we can attribute to Ionians in the Greek West was in
a different sphere – that of intellectual and spiritual values.
Here we can be in no doubt of either the source or the signifi⁄
cance of the Ionic contribution; for we are in the presence of
some of the most illustrious figures in the history of Greek
thought.

The most celebrated personality among these Ionic emigrants
was Pythagoras, who is said to have left Samos about 530 BC
and settled at Croton in southern Italy. There is little doubt
that Pythagoras was a brilliant mathematician. He discovered
the extraordinary fact that the harmonic intervals of the octave
have a numerical ratio, and it was almost certainly he who
later made the disconcerting discovery of irrational square roots.
It was unfortunate that Pythagoras' two great advances in
knowledge were made in this order, because the first led him to
invent an elaborate explanation of the universe in terms of
numbers (the unit being a point with the minimum of magni⁄
tude), and the second discovery showed that in a universe of
such a structure there is no place for the diagonal of a square of
measurable side. This inescapable dilemma may have been the
main reason why a curtain of secrecy was drawn in front of the
doctrines taught in Pythagoras' school. As a result, little is
known of the master's personal contributions to knowledge.
But they must have been considerable; indeed, Empedocles the

Sicilian said Pythagoras could see anything if he really gave his mind to it.

This is only one aspect of Pythagoras' mental activity. Being a Samian, he was brought up in an atmosphere of opportunism that prepared him for exercising his remarkable talents among the unintellectual Western Greeks. He was not only a scholar but a prophet; and, preaching a doctrine of the reincarnation of souls, he formed a huge brotherhood at Croton that wielded political power in his lifetime and lasted as a mathematical and religious school for a century or more after his death. Success evidently emboldened him, and an ancient critic tells us that, while in early life he was a serious scholar, in his later years he could not resist the temptation to work miracles. He pointed out things that he remembered from previous incarnations; and an older refugee from Ionia, Xenophanes, who had a clear head and was not inclined to treat the new prophet with honour, satirised his showmanship in a scathing epigram: one day (he said), passing a man who was beating a puppy, Pythagoras shouted out, 'Stop your flogging! I tell you, this is the soul of an old friend of mine, which I recognise by its cries.' To us the Pythagorean system appears a bran-tub of mystical notions and superstitious taboos. At Ephesus his contemporary Heraclitus was not at all favourably impressed by what he heard; for he accused Pythagoras of dishonesty in his researches and scornfully remarked that much learning had not taught him sense. But later generations revered Pythagoras, and many anecdotes and comments in ancient writers testify to the high standard of morality that was expected of his followers.

The second school, or movement, of Ionic speculation in the West flourished among the weather-beaten Phocaeans who had settled at Elea in Italy about the same time as Pythagoras arrived at Croton; in time, this school belongs rather to the next generation. The weapon of the Eleatics was *reductio ad absurdum*. The negative force of their arguments appears most trenchantly in the paradoxes by which Zeno demonstrated that in a universe composed of a finite number of points, such as the Pythagoreans envisaged, Achilles could never overtake a tortoise in a race, and an arrow in flight must at any given moment be at rest. The paradoxes were a challenge rather than a positive contention; it is not that the arrow, for instance, does not actually reach its mark, but that the underlying conception of space is false. The fourth paradox, if the explanation given here is correct, shows best what Zeno was trying to do.

Fig. 35

Zeno was the pupil of a remarkable thinker named Parmenides, whose reputation is based on a poem in which he expounded the Truth without regard for the accumulated experience of the senses. Parmenides thought out his argument, about the beginning of the fifth century, as a challenge to existing theories; and he used the old poetic diction with originality to dramatise a masterpiece of tough reasoning which led to conclusions as perverse as Zeno's paradoxes. Justifying himself by the old plea of divine revelation, Parmenides affirmed that the one true road of knowledge is 'is, and cannot not be' – or

Fig. 35. Zeno's Fourth Paradox. The letters represent continuous series of points of minimum magnitude, which are supposedly indivisible. The A row is stationary on a track, the B and Γ rows are moving in opposite directions at equal velocity. The object of the paradox seems to be this: a point in the B row passing from one point to the next in the A row moves an indivisible minimum unit of space in an indivisible minimum unit of time; but while the leading point of the B row is passing half of the A row, the leading point of the Γ row will have traversed the whole length of the B row and so have passed twice as many indivisible points. According to Aristotle, Zeno's conclusion is that the half is equal to twice itself. But the true aim of the paradox must be to demonstrate that the supposedly indivisible unit is divisible after all

words to that effect. The point is not easily made in English, because, if we say '*What is,* is,' we limit the range of our remark, and if we say '*It* is,' we expose ourselves to the decisive retort, 'Yes, but the other isn't.' The statement 'is' must be regarded as completely general. What Parmenides was determined to establish was that existence is the one thing that is real, and the whole notion of 'not being' disappears without trace; for, he says, you could not recognise or point out the non-existent (he, of course, had the advantage that there was no figure o in the Greek numeral systems). Having established this premise as the only valid one, Parmenides was then able to proceed by logical argument and rule out all possibility of growth and decay, movement or change.

Parmenides naturally did not believe that these conclusions were the real truth; and he did in fact compose a second part to his poem in which he gave what he calls an 'illusory' account of the universe. His main argument was in fact a challenge to existing beliefs; it was the reaction of a keen young ascetic who had not been trained in a scientific school and asserted his intellectual power by streamlined abstract reasoning. But, like the paradoxes, it had a positive force. Turned the other way round, it proved that things like plurality and motion, if they are admitted to exist, cannot have been spontaneously gener-ated; they must always have been present. Consequently, his argument could not be overlooked, and it compelled a re-thinking of existing theories.

In diamond-cut-diamond logic of this sort academic Miletus had no interest; her leading scientist at this time was in any case most distinguished as a geographer and cartographer. But to match the Samian and Phocaean thinkers abroad, the less liberal city of Ephesus produced a brilliant intellectual at home. This was the blue-blooded Heraclitus, whom later generations named the Obscure. He was the successor of the Milesian physicists to this extent, that he felt it necessary to make one of the elements – in this case fire – the paramount substance in his universe. But he was really more impressed by problems like perpetual change and the balance and counter-tension of opposites; and he too had a flair for paradoxical statements. His work is known only in isolated apophthegms, some of which were misapplied by the Stoics when they revived them in a later age. They show a new insistence on 'cleverness'; but they are random remarks taken out of their context, and they have little more coherence than the table conversation of Martin Luther, so that (as Theophrastus saw) one should not look for consistency in them.

In Heraclitus' view, intelligence does not consist in accumu-lating knowledge but in a more or less intuitive understanding of the sum of things; and systematic observation of nature thus ceases to be the essential basis of speculation. When human souls are to be distinguished, the distinction is between 'wet' and 'dry' ones; the dry, being more ethereal, are 'cleverer and better', and water is death to them. This in itself could still be a scientific hypothesis. But there is also a hint in the apoph-thegms that souls will not receive equal treatment after death: some of them – presumably the few dry ones – seem likely to fare better than the others; and if this is so, physical science has ceased to be a disinterested study.

The thinkers of this generation were overstepping the limits of reasoned enquiry; they were no longer scientists, but (to use Pythagoras' own word) 'philosophers'. This may have been the greatest turning-point in the history of Greek thought. To us Pythagoras may seem a charlatan, and Heraclitus something of a bigot. But these qualities were inherent in their age; for per-sonality and cleverness were commanding greater attention in Greece, and everywhere – except perhaps in Ionia – people were feeling the need of spiritual experience or personal re-assurance. Milesian science did not in fact die out. Miletus itself suffered a crushing blow; but the last of the line of the old

Fig. 36. The World of Hecataeus, about 500 BC. (After Klausen.) The belief that Hecataeus' world was disk-shaped and surrounded by Ocean depends on a criticism that Herodotus levelled against his own predecessors. Hecataeus included Libya (i.e. Africa) in the continent of Asia and seems to have made Asia and Europe equal in size. He wrote a Description of the World which contained many hundreds of place-names

Ionic thinkers in the fifth century seem, as we shall presently see, to have derived their scientific method from the cool atmosphere of Milesian rationalism. In the meantime, however, more specialised studies were gaining ground. Medicine and physical sensation began to be systematically investigated, together with embryology and experiments in vivisection; and a wing of the Pythagorean school continued the master's abstruse mathe-matical researches. Astronomy remained part of physical science, but terrestrial geography was studied for its own sake; before the destruction of Miletus, Hecataeus travelled in Egypt and wrote a guide to the earth, and he drew up a portable map *Fig. 36* which contained a great deal more detail than Anaximander's original one.

If Pythagoras was the most spectacular of Samians in the   THE SAMOS West, the most spectacular Samian at home was Polycrates. He   OF succeeded to a despotism that had perhaps been set up by his   POLYCRATES father; and since the islands had not been conquered by the Persians, he owed allegiance to no one. Polycrates was the one Greek ruler at this time who understood that sea power, if effectively used, was equal to the land forces of a great kingdom. Under his rule, Samian squadrons were equally active in battle, privateering and levying tolls; they captured enemy transports and seized or held to ransom other Aegean cities; and in the pursuit of his political aims Polycrates made and broke treaties with the rulers of Egypt and the Persian empire until he was lured to his death by the prospect of even greater success. His reign is an outstanding example of political opportunism.

To play a rôle of this sort Samos needed secure defences. Polycrates therefore enclosed the city in a strong circuit wall *Fig. 37* running along the mountain crest at the back; on the west side, where engines could be brought against it, he had his Mytilen-aean prisoners cut a fosse 18 feet wide in the rock. He himself occupied a fortified citadel, probably on the promontory that shields the harbour. To ensure the safety of his fleet, we are told, he constructed a mole a couple of furlongs long in 20 fathoms of water and made ship-sheds for his galleys. The area enclosed in the city circuit was about three-quarters of a mile square, and so was large enough for a great population. Herodotus speaks

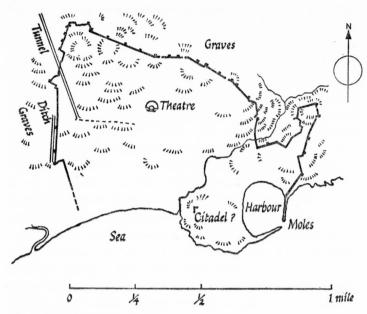

Fig. 37. Plan of Polycrates' city of Samos

of Polycrates' Samos as being the first of cities in Greece and foreign lands.

In one respect this new city was incomplete; it lacked running water. Now, the tyrants in the Greek cities paid special attention to water supply; at Athens water was piped to nine fountains in the city, and at Megara also a water system had been constructed. Polycrates decided to execute an even bolder engineering feat and (like Hezekiah at Jerusalem) to bring water into the city from a spring in the valley on the far side of the mountain crest. He summoned an engineer from Megara, called Eupalinus; and, with great efforts, the task was successfully completed. The water was brought in pipes to the back of the mountain, and from there it flowed through a tunnel

1,100 yards long to emerge at length inside the city. In the
heart of the mountain it was piped at the bottom of a tile-   Plate 35
covered channel 2 or 3 feet wide, with a rather broader raised
gangway-shelf running alongside; but, owing perhaps to a
miscalculation of the flow of the water, the channel had in part
to be cut to a depth of 30 feet from the roof. The tunnel was
excavated simultaneously from both ends. We cannot say precisely what calculations were made for gauging the relative
height of the two cuttings; but the fact that the vertical error
in the middle of the tunnel was only a few feet (nine by
Fabricius' account) would suggest accurate levelling, and in
fact the invention of the level, together with other instruments,
was ascribed in antiquity to the Samian engineer, Theodorus.
These works mark the end of an epoch. Like his city lay-out,
Polycrates' engineering feats were so much in advance of their
time that nearly 100 years later Herodotus could still speak of
them as the greatest works in existence among the Greeks.

Polycrates was trapped and crucified at Magnesia by the
rebellious satrap Oroites about 522 BC; and soon after that
came the disaster. Polycrates' power was left in the hands of his
secretary Maeandrius. This man had no stomach for autocratic
rule. He summoned an assembly of the citizens and offered, on
condition of some personal safeguards, to restore equality of
political rights. Thereupon a quick-tempered burgher stood up
and abused him, exclaiming that he was of mean birth and a
pest anyway, and that he ought rather to render an account of
the monies he had handled. So Maeandrius repented of his
offer, and retiring once more to the citadel he began to rule as a
tyrant. Now, there was a brother of Polycrates named Syloson
who had been banished from Samos. He happened to visit
Egypt as a tourist about 525 BC at the time when the Persians
invaded the country; and when a young Persian officer in the
market place of Memphis admired his red cloak and wanted to
buy it, the proud Samian gave it him as a present. He gave no

more thought to the matter; but when Maeandrius set himself up as tyrant in Samos and the young officer had meanwhile become King of Persia, Syloson went up to Susa and asked for his recompense. Darius gave him a contingent of Persians, and he returned and landed in Samos. The Samians at once came to terms with him. Maeandrius himself packed his trunks and escaped by a secret passage that led down from his citadel to the water's edge; but his hot-headed young brother armed the palace guard and without warning cut down the Persian grandees as they sat in their sedan chairs. Incensed by this outrage, the Persian troops set to work to kill the inhabitants of Samos, and after dragging the island with nets they handed it back desolate to Syloson. Thus Samian world power ended in catastrophe. As an Ionic versifier put it

'There's lots of room now, thanks to Syloson.'

The turn of Miletus was not long delayed. Aristagoras, the acting boss there, seems to have been as imprudent as he was ambitious. He quarrelled with the Persian governor in Ionia, and in 499 BC he raised the Eastern Greeks in revolt. A commando from Ephesus burnt Sardis and made reconciliation impossible; and Persian armies were despatched to the West. After four or five years of hard fighting the Persians closed in on Miletus by land and sea. In a desperate effort the Greeks of the coast mustered a fleet of 363 vessels and engaged the 600 galleys of the Persian grand fleet. Defeated in front of Miletus, they had no further defence. Miletus was destroyed; the remnant of its inhabitants was transported into exile at Ampe on the Persian Gulf, and the rest of the coast, together with the neighbouring islands, was reduced to subjection.

CHAPTER X

Between Athens and Persia

ONLY FIFTEEN YEARS after the Ionian Revolt the cities of Eastern Greece rose in rebellion a second time. But this time the Persians were on the defensive. In 480 BC the full muster of the imperial Persian forces had invaded Greece and been repelled; in 479 Greek victory was clinched by the Battle of Plataea, and a second action at the mountain foot opposite Miletus allowed the East Aegean cities to recover their freedom, together with a share of military glory. Thanks to the foresight of Themistocles, the Athenians had gained naval supremacy in the Aegean; and they set to work to form an anti-Persian confederacy in which the Greek cities of the East readily joined as allies. In the first twenty years or so of this league the Athenians, together with their allies, drove the Persians out of Europe, overwhelmed a new armada on the Eurymedon river in Pamphylia, and carried the war to Cyprus and the Nile. The response to Athenian leadership was enthusiastic.

In time, however, the character of the league began to change. From the outset Athens had been the dominant partner. Gradually she became the mistress. For convenience, most of the cities had compounded for their share of fleet maintenance by monetary payments; presently they found themselves in the position of tributaries, and states which attempted to secede were punished as revolting subjects. There are several inscriptions which show that in the middle of the fifth century Athens was interfering in the internal government of the Ionic cities, establishing democracy after her own pattern and appointing her own commissioners. Samos had kept up her sea-power, and (apart from the battle off Miletus) there had been scarcely a sea-fight during 100 years without the Samian squadrons earning special mention by their gallantry. But when

Samos quarrelled with Miletus in 441 BC, Athens intervened and after a long struggle overpowered the island-city. And later, when the Mytilenaeans tried to break away from the league, their city was captured by siege and their territory was divided into lots for Athenian settlers. Until it began to disintegrate after the Athenian debacle in Sicily (413 BC) the league was in effect an Athenian empire, paying tribute for Athens to use for whatever purpose she wished, and it ceased even to be anti-Persian when in the mid fifth century a private covenant between Athens and the King removed the danger of a full-scale Persian offensive.

It would be idle to blame Athens for this change of attitude. Imperialism never entirely lacks for justification; and there is no doubt that the adherents of democracy in many of the subject cities were glad of the support that Athens afforded them. Even after the Athenian disaster of 413 BC, when the league was breaking up, there was no lack of people in Ionia who remained faithful in sentiment to Athens; and, curiously, when Athens was reduced to the most desperate straits, the populace of Samos proved itself more Athenian than the Athenians themselves. Nevertheless, the fact remains that in the era of the Athenian league Ionic city life was at its lowest ebb. Archaeologically, it is virtually non-existent: no substantial new buildings seem to have been erected, Ionic art was at an end, and the sites of the eastern Aegean cities show scarcely any sign of urban habitation in this period. What the Ionic democrats judged to be best for themselves was evidently not what was best for Ionia.

The ancient writers tell us little enough about the history of eastern Greece and nothing whatever about conditions there in the fifth century. But we may infer two distinct consequences of Athenian rule. On the one hand, though the cities had recovered their freedom, the Persian land-survey continued in force; so the cities, as corporate bodies, belonged to the Athenian league and paid their tribute, but the landowners seem to have paid rent to the Persian overlord for their estates. The Greeks of the Asiatic coast thus found themselves serving two masters. The landowners must maintain good relations with satraps and grandees, and there were times when demo⁄ cratic pressure instigated by Athens drove them into the arms of the Persians. In some of the cities the result of this inter⁄ ference was an embitterment of political strife which did not end with the collapse of the Athenian empire.

The other serious consequence of Athenian rule concerned the economic life of the cities. The Greeks of the eastern Aegean had suffered disaster in the Ionian revolt; and in the normal way it might have taken them a generation or so to recover their economic prosperity. But prosperity does not seem to have returned under Athenian rule. We know that in the Black Sea Athens refounded the Ionic city of Amisus as an Athenian colony under the new name of Piraeus; and we can only suppose that, as too easily happens, liberation and economic exploitation went hand in hand and trade tended to go to Athens rather than to Ionia. Athenian financial control of the league has now been spot⁄lighted by the discovery of copies of an Athenian decree in which the minting of silver by the allied cities was forbidden. Athens in effect became the capital of empire; and the subject cities, though nominally free, sank to the condition of towns whose function was to supply the capital. To the Greeks of the eastern Aegean there was no longer opportunity at home; bright lads – not to mention girls like Aspasia – who wanted to make a career or acquire a reputation must move in to Athens to live without civic rights, or they must travel further afield outside the Athenian empire. We must therefore follow our Ionians abroad, and we may begin with a glance at the Persian Empire.

The Persian Empire was ruled by one man, the King. In the sky Dyaosh (whom the Greeks called Zeus, the Romans

THE PERSIAN EMPIRE

123

Jupiter) ruled as supreme god; he was 'Ahura' (Lord) and 'Mazda' (Wise), and by his grace the King was absolute ruler of Parsa. No matter what struggles there might be for the succession, the ruler at any given moment was an autocrat by divine right. Before Cyrus conquered Astyages in the 550's the Persians were one of the peoples of the Median empire, which after the fall of Nineveh in 612 BC had come to extend from the River Halys in Asia Minor to Kabul in the East; but after Cyrus' victory they became the senior partners in empire. Within 50 years of his accession fresh territory on every frontier had been 'grabbed' (to use the Persians' own word), and the King's writ prevailed from Cyrenaica and Elephantine to the Jaxartes, and from the Indus to what is now the Bulgarian coast. The efficient organisation of this enormous realm was the work of one man, Darius, who by his ruthless determination, or (as Herodotus relates) through the uninhibited behaviour of his horse, secured the throne for himself in 522 BC. Under Darius the empire was divided into upwards of 20 provinces, each ruled by a 'satrap'. The satraps were both civil and military governors, and normally they were Persians or Medes of high rank; so long as they remitted the tribute of their satrapies and provided military levies, they were usually allowed a free hand. At the same time, Median and Persian nobles received great estates as fiefs from the King, and many of them became grandees in the provinces.

The resources of the empire were canalised by Darius in an elaborate fiscal system in which the King became sole proprietor of the vast profit-making concern. The annual tribute alone amounted to three and a half million gold pounds, and this had a much greater real value than the corresponding sum at the present day. The King issued the imperial currency, consisting of gold staters (Darics, or 'archers') and silver shekels (*sigloi*), both of which bore his image; and the reputation of this currency, together with the facilities for travel in the empire,

Fig. 38. Royal Persian silver shekel, the King as archer. The currency continued with little change from 516 BC to 331 BC

encouraged the expansion of trade. Before he grew old, Darius seems to have led his armed forces in person, and his son Xerxes commanded the great expedition to Greece in 480 B C; but it was partly at least the result of Darius' system that later rulers tended to be rooted to their imperial capitals and to live their lives as secluded sultans imprisoned in an orbit of palace etiquette and harem intrigues.

The Persians had been a mountain people of simple habits and tastes. Their feudal aristocracy was trained to ride, to shoot, and to tell the truth; and they had little formal education. Con-sequently they lacked the abilities necessary for administering a vast empire. Native officials continued to form the civil ser-vice under the satraps in the provinces. The *lingua franca* for communications in the empire was Aramaic, the accounts of the royal household were kept in the Elamite language and signary. Mercantile procedure was Babylonian. Greeks were preferred as court doctors. A Carian named Scylax was sent by Darius down the Indus to explore the coasts round to Suez. Phoenicians and in a lesser degree Egyptians formed the admiralty on the Mediterranean; and in the later days of the empire the shock-troops were Greek hoplites. Even Darius' imperial law-code was little more than a re-hash of the 1250-year-old judgements of Hammurabi.

Cyrus had taken over the Median capital of Hagmatana (Ecbatana, now Hamadan), while in winter he moved down to hold his court in Babylon. But Hagmatana was far away in the Median highlands, and Babylon was alien and tumultuous. Darius planted his capital at the old Elamite city of Susa, and his account of its building merits a few words. As he himself tells us, the laying of foundations and making of the bricks were the work of Babylonians; cedars were felled in the Lebanon and brought by Assyrians to Babylon, thence to Susa by Carians and Ionians; teak (or some such timber) came from Gandhara and Carmania, gold from Sardis and

from Bactria, lapis lazuli and carnelian from Sogdiana, tur-
quoise (or some other dull stone) from Chorasmia, and silver
and 'stone-wood' (perhaps ebony) from Egypt; the ornamenta-
tion of the walls was brought from Ionia; ivory came from
Ethiopia, India and Arachosia, the stone pillars from a neighbouring village of Elam; Ionians and Lydians were the stone-
carvers; Medes and Egyptians were the goldsmiths, and they
too adorned the walls; Lydians and Egyptians did the woodwork; and Ionians resident in Babylonia made the baked
bricks or tiles. From this record we see that Darius' new palace
was a monument of imperial collaboration. But it was symptomatic of another aspect of Persian rule. Everything flowed in to
the centre. But nothing radiated outwards. There was no
Persian civilisation, no Persian secular art or culture, no common bond of language or literature, nothing in fact that could
give the various peoples of the empire the feeling that they
belonged together.

Susa is stifling in summer, and the prestige of empire required a new capital in Persia itself. So Darius began, and his
successors completed, a huge new palace in the Persian mountains. He named it Parsa, and the Greeks called it Persepolis.
It was built on terraces to which access was given by grand
converging staircases. Both at Susa and at Persepolis the
audience chamber, or 'apadana', was a great, dimly-lit hall
supported by 36 columns and filled with trophies from the
conquered nations. The magnificence of the palaces signified
the boundlessness of the empire, the trophies underlined the
futility of struggling against so omnipotent a ruler.

Darius has told us that at Susa the stone-carvers were
Ionians and Lydians; and both there and at Persepolis the
huge columns reared their heads in a sort of rococo Ionic
splendour. At Susa the walls were faced with glazed tiles
which portrayed a protective array of monsters and guardsmen
Plate 36   in painted relief – the frieze of archers, now in the Louvre,

displays Ionic art in the service of the imperial master. The
promenade of the apadana of Persepolis was lined with carved
stone friezes; and a great series depicted the New Year's Day
spectacle of the Persian empire, in which guards, files of alternating Persians and Medes, and long ranks of subject peoples
with their offerings all advanced in procession to pay homage
to the King. There must have been a good few Greek artisans
engaged on this work; and the master who adapted their in-
bred idioms to the cosmopolitan pageantry of Persian imperialism must have been an artist of considerable creative
vision, comparable to the designer of the Parthenon frieze at
Athens. We read in the Elder Pliny of a sculptor, Telephanes,
of Phocis or more probably Ionic Phocaea, whom the experts
had ranked among the greatest of all Greek sculptors, but of
whose work nothing was known because, as it was said, his
career was largely spent in the workshops of Xerxes and
Darius; and we thus in all probability know the name of the
grand master of the Persepolis friezes.

Plate 37

Plate 38

In an empire such as this, good communications were
needed. The 'Royal Road' from Sardis to Susa was about
1,600 miles long, with 111 posting stations; and it was reckoned
a three-month journey for ordinary travellers. But it was a
regular trunk road; and not only Greek artisans, but Greek
exiles and embassies passed along it. With a price on his head,
and disguised as a woman, Themistocles trundled along this
road in a curtained coach after he had been banished from
Athens; and though it was to him above all others that the
defeat of the Persians in 480 BC had been due, he did not
hesitate to seek refuge at the Persian court. It may be straining
credulity too far to accept Plutarch's tale that the King paid
over to Themistocles the reward that had been offered for his
capture; but he was certainly received with signal honour. He
learned Persian and lived as a landed gentleman on an estate
given him by Artaxerxes I; and it is related that once, when

he saw a great repast prepared for himself and his family, he mentally compared this surfeit with his simple life at Athens before he was exiled and cried 'Oh boys! we should be ruined if we had not been ruined.'

We know of other Greek exiles who received big estates; and Eastern Greeks were promoted to positions of high authority in the empire, among them a Halicarnassian who was made satrap of Cilicia. Ctesias of Cnidus was court doctor at the end of the fifth century and was employed as envoy on a special diplomatic mission. He took advantage of his situation to write a history of Persia and an account of India; and though we must impute to him a great deal more fable than truth, we are indebted to him for our knowledge of the intrigues of the Persian court.

Peace reigned in the Asiatic empire in the mid fifth century. Conditions for travel were at their best; and it was possible then for a gentleman of Halicarnassus to move freely about Egypt, Babylonia and the Levant, as well as to visit the Scythians, lecture in Athens and Olympia, and participate in the foundation of a new Athenian colony in Italy. This man was the historian Herodotus. His travels were part of a grand programme of research. He set himself the task of composing a history of the wars between Greeks and Persians. But he realised that the causes of the struggle must be traced back to their beginnings; and, in a work that would fill four volumes such as this, he sketched the history of the various peoples concerned. He did not confine himself to the simple narrative of events. To him 'History', whose original meaning was simply 'enquiry' or 'research', included the geography of the known world, together with natural history and the social organisation, customs and religious practices of the different races. In reading Herodotus we are conscious of breadth of understanding, curiosity, scepticism and tolerance blended in a way that would be impossible without foreign travel. Herodotus was without a rival as a historian, whether in his scholarly interests or his literary gifts. But there must have been other Eastern Greeks who acquired something of the same grasp of world affairs and glimpsed a wider horizon than that of the routine rivalries of Athens and Sparta. This is the reason why later, in the new Oriental world of Alexander the Great and his successors, so many Eastern Greeks found themselves promoted to positions of high responsibility.

For Ionians who left home in the hope of earning a livelihood as teachers or men of marketable skills Athens under Pericles was the principal focus. Many of these emigrants became professional men or public figures with a reputation to sustain, and if there was a single quality that united them it was common sense. Most notable among them were the intellectuals, the range of whose curiosity covered physical science, the development of societies and the working of the human body.

IONIC
SCIENCE

Of all the Greek thinkers of the fifth century perhaps the most acute was Anaxagoras. He was a citizen of Clazomenae in Northern Ionia, and he lived for many years in Athens in the second quarter or middle of the century; Pericles was an enthusiastic pupil of his. If, as is said, Anaxagoras studied natural science at Miletus, it is easy to understand why he was preoccupied with the problem of air. Air is 'strong' – that is to say, it has body – as Anaxagoras demonstrated by tying up empty wine skins and squeezing them. But the distance from the earth to the heavenly bodies was evidently enormous, and the thin disk of the earth seemed to occupy very little of the total space of the universe. If, as Parmenides claimed, there was no void, the amount of air must vastly exceed that of all other substances. Anaxagoras therefore assumed that in the original state of the universe before the separating-off process began, air must have preponderated to such an extent that the minute particles of other substances would simply not have been perceptible. This question of the perceptibility of minority particles was fundamental to his thought; and he carried out other experiments, such as pouring one fluid drop by drop into another to find the limit at which our senses begin to take note of change.

On the basis of his observations Anaxagoras was able to work out a theory of matter. Everything contains minute particles of everything else in varying proportions, and the old difficulty of one substance changing into another presents no problem. Food, for instance, contains imperceptible particles of bone and hair which are sorted out in our digestive processes. Intelligence, on the other hand, cannot be apprehended by our senses, not even in the way that we can apprehend air; it must therefore be most subtle in substance, not mixing with other substances. In animate creatures it is portions of Intelligence that dictate movement; and it must therefore be Intelligence that started the cosmic movement by which the different sub-stances began to be separated out. At the same time, Anax-agoras recognised that this cosmic vortex, in which the heavenly bodies revolve with increasing acceleration, is, generally speak-ing, fore-ordained, and so – to Plato's great disgust – the uni-versal Intelligence in Anaxagoras' system was hardly more than a cranking device to get the machine running.

Anaxagoras' brilliance is most evident in his celestial science. He realised, as Anaximander had not done, that the stars are further away than the sun, and the moon is nearer. He gave good rational explanations of meteorites, the rainbow and eclipses. Above all, he recognised that the moon shines with reflected light, and so he was able to sweep away the old theory that the heavenly bodies are opaque tubes with nozzles through which the incandescence shows. The luminaries of the sky could now be solid bodies – the moon a land with plains and chasms, the sun a lump of red-hot metal or stone. In contrast to the philosophers, who found a spherical earth more in keep-ing with their notions of perfect form, Anaxagoras adhered to the old Milesian view that the earth is flat. This, after all, was the common-sense view; for elementary geometry would show that with a spherical earth the distance of the sun and size of the earth must exceed all reasonable limits. He was then able to calculate the size of the sun. This was presumably done in two stages: first a calculation of the sun's distance by triangulation on a north-south baseline (e.g. Miletus-Memphis), whose length would of course have to be estimated; and secondly by simple experiment to determine the ratio of the sun's diameter to its distance from the eye. Anaxagoras was inaccurate in his observations. He claimed that the sun was larger than the Peloponnese, which by Greek standards of measurement would mean at least five days' journey across its disk; and with the use of an atlas we can demonstrate that if his data had been correct, he should have reckoned it less than three. But his great achievement consisted in attempting the calculation.

Scientific observations of this sort would not have caused public offence in Miletus 150 years earlier. But the Athens of Sophocles could not take it. Anaxagoras was prosecuted for his blasphemous assertions about the heavenly bodies, and, like Socrates after him, he was found guilty. But the great man's memory did not pass unhonoured. In the Ionic city of Lampsacus, to which he retired, the school-children, in accordance with his special request, were given a holiday every year in the month of his death.

Of the other scientists of this age, Melissus is most famous as the Samian admiral who defeated Pericles' fleet in 441 BC and enabled Samos to defy Athens for a time. But he also turned his attention to philosophy and defended Parmenides' theory against an attack that had developed. On the assumption that motion does in fact exist, it had been pointed out that movement inside Parmenides' finite spherical One must cause a bulge, and the idea of a lop-sided One was little short of ridiculous; Melissus therefore concluded that the spherical One must be infinite and incorporeal. But an altogether more startling product of Ionic imagination was the Atomic system, which was later adopted by Epicurus and has taken its place in world literature through the great poem of Lucretius. The inventor of the theory, Leucippus, may have been a Milesian. But it was Democritus who developed its full implications in the generation after Anaxagoras. Democritus was a descendant of the Ionic emigrants from Teos who formed a colony at Abdera in Thrace. He is said to have travelled widely in the East, and he wrote many books on a variety of topics. He was later called the 'laughing philosopher' because of the emphasis that he placed on good humour in his moral teaching.

The lack of a glass industry in Greece at this time was a major handicap. Without microscopes the ancient scientists could do no more than theorise about the constitution of mat-ter below the level of unaided vision. And the Atomic theory therefore did not represent an advance on Anaxagoras resulting from closer observation, but was an alternative explanation of the mechanism of nature to fit the known data. Primarily, the Atomists differed from Anaxagoras in their attitude towards Parmenidean logic. Space, in their view, was infinitely divis-ible; but the atoms of which matter is composed were indivis-ible and impenetrable bodies. The atoms were thus the in-divisible minimum units of physical substance, but they did not constitute space. To give them freedom of movement, the atomists had to defy Parmenides and re-affirm the belief in empty space; and thus their two basic realities were 'the full' (or 'built-up') and 'the void' (which, properly speaking, does not exist). In themselves, the atoms were all of the same substance; but they differed in shape, position and arrange-ment, and these differences accounted for the multiplicity of phenomena. The creation of our world started with large num-bers of atoms breaking off from the infinite mass and going into a huddle in a patch of empty space. A vortex was set up; the process of separation commenced; and, with the frequent colli-sions that occurred, larger groupings of matter were built up by the entanglement of atoms. The question what prompted the process of creation is not clearly answered, though – once begun – the process is automatic and the driving force is 'Necessity'. It may have been with a view to pre-empting this question that the Atomists postulated innumerable worlds of different shapes and sizes which are constantly coming into being and dissolv-ing, or being destroyed by collision with one another.

There are some crudities in the system, especially in the Atomists' theory of knowledge and sense-perception; and 'automatic' motion could of course be pressed to the point where human free-will is ruled out in favour of materialistic determinism. This aspect of Atomism must have been re-pugnant to Plato, and it may account for the fact that Demo-critus is never once mentioned in all his writings. But Anax-agoras and the Atomists mark the peak of Greek constructive thought about nature. For, apart from advances in mathe-matics, little more could be done without scientific instruments. It was symptomatic of the change which was coming that by this time Sicily had produced its own mystic, and other Greek thinkers began to appear who were not Ionians in origin. Drawing strength from the sophistic movement, Athenian philosophers were working round to a notion that true know-ledge comes from inside us, the test of its validity being in effect to circumvent a real or imaginary opponent in argument. Inevitably the evidence of the senses was dethroned; and the consequence is summed up in the words of an Ionic thinker who makes the indignant sense-organs protest to the mind, 'You wretch, you get all your evidence from us and you will throw us over. Our overthrow will be your downfall.'

If the study of the laws of nature was important, the study of evolution was almost more so. The historian Diodorus has preserved a theory of man's beginnings which must go back to the fifth-century Ionians. The origins of life and evolution of species need not detain us here, because there was nothing to add to what Anaximander had worked out a century earlier. The interest lies rather in the sketch of man's early development. At first he was a lone food-cropper. But presently human beings started to band themselves together for protection, and in due course such groups of people developed the faculty of speech. In this way different languages arose. Gradually men learned to clothe themselves and look for shelter, and then to store food and to cultivate it. Finally, with the discovery of fire, various handicrafts were invented. Necessity, at every stage, was the teacher, and experience was the basis of progress; but man was an apter pupil than the animals because of his hands and quick wits and the power of articulate speech.

The true significance of this account of human beginnings may not at first be fully evident. It only appears when we consider its effect on established belief – if for instance we were brought up to believe that Justice is divine, that law and social order are fore-ordained, that all change is for the worse, or that gods existed in the likeness of civilised human beings before man was created. Seen in this light it is one of the greatest achievements of Ionic rational thought. And more than one research viewpoint was needed to give it its full perspective: to take a single example, the conception of a development of society could hardly have been formulated until the predecessors of Herodotus had studied primitive communities on the fringes of the civilised world. At the same time, this sketch has so much in common with known opinions of Anaxagoras and the Atomists that we must suppose that it reflects their general views on evolution.

These ideas were not of course the monopoly of the natural scientists. One of the great teachers of the mid fifth century, Protagoras, who also came from Abdera, taught that 'man is the measure of all things'; and presumably he went on to argue that society and institutions have been evolved by human communities and should therefore be adapted to fit their needs. Protagoras taught Virtue – by which he may have meant social behaviour based on a science of government and conduct that can be learned; and the reputation he gained in Athens was such that in 444 B C he was engaged to draft a law-code for the new Athenian colony of Thurii in southern Italy. This Periclean foundation had very distinguished beginnings. The historian Herodotus also joined in the enterprise; and the importance attached to the physical lay-out of the city is shown by the presence there of a Milesian scientist, Hippodamus, who was particularly celebrated for his pioneer work in city-planning. Thurii was thus symbolic of the practical application of Ionic thought; for the experience gained from the scientific study of evolution, history and environment was harnessed to planning a better future.

We have seen that in the fifth century the Ionic thinkers and professional men were active everywhere except in Ionia. But one science – that of healing – was quietly developed at home in the eastern Aegean. The most progressive movement in medicine at this time seems to have been that of the Asclepiads at Cnidus and Cos; and a great body of Ionic writings, which is known to us as the 'Hippocratic Corpus', illuminates the work of an experimental movement which was distinguished by a rational attitude towards diseases and treatment, as well as by insistence on accurate observation of symptoms. The name of Hippocrates of Cos, who was active in the second half of the fifth century, is inseparably linked with the history of the Coan school of medicine. Unfortunately, as with Pythagoras' mathematical discoveries, modern scholars have not been able to form a clear estimate of the master's own personal contribution, and some deny him any share in the 'Hippocratic' writings. In Plato's view, Hippocrates' eminence rested upon his grasp of the metaphysic of organisms. But the Hippocratic writings at least are characterised by a professional contempt for the *a priori* notions of philosophers who theorise about the human body; and it seems therefore best to disregard Plato's views and suppose that Hippocrates was honoured not as a theorist but because he devoted his serious attention to his patients and was not ashamed of soiling his hands in clinical practice.

CHAPTER XI

The Fourth-century Revival

THE FIFTH CENTURY proved to be a turning-point in the history of the Mediterranean world. In 480–79 BC the Carthaginians had been checked in Sicily and the combined land and sea forces of the Persian Empire had been repelled from the Aegean, with the result that the Greeks were supreme in all the regions that they had colonised. But before the end of the fifth century the tide began to ebb. This may to a limited extent have been due to diminishing military effectiveness and vigour among the citizens of the outlying Greek cities. But a greater part in the decline must have been played by the opposition of two irreconcilable ideologies centred on Athens and Sparta. Few parts of the Greek world remained unaffected by this pernicious rivalry; and far too great a proportion of the total resources and effort of the Greek cities was consumed in the catastrophic struggle which engulfed contending parties and states. In the meantime, the Carthaginians bit off half of Sicily; tough native tribes closed in on the colonies of southern Gaul and Italy, and the Greeks lost their foothold in Campania. To the north of the Aegean the storm was gathering. The Thracians were pinning the Greek settlements against the Hellespont; and the Ionic colonies on the Asiatic coast of the Black Sea felt the menace of militant Paphlagonian nationalism and the hostility of Colchian tribesmen.

In the East the Persian King had ceased to be formidable. But he had not ceased to be rich; and individually the leading states of the Greek mainland courted him, much as impecunious nephews will court a wealthy uncle who promises, and occasionally disburses, largess to those who do what he tells them. In the early fourth century there were statesmen in Greece who realised that with one concerted effort the Greeks could overthrow his empire, or at least annex its western provinces. But by that time the King had become the umpire of Greek politics; and there were always Greek states or parties to whom the preservation of 'Sick Man' Persia was a matter of political necessity.

The Spartans traded the Greek cities of Asia to the King in exchange for Persian aid in the war against Athens. But neither they nor the satrap Tissaphernes honoured the bargain; and it was the ambitious natures of Lysander and Cyrus the Younger that eventually made the alliance a success. Cyrus was the second son of Darius II but the favourite of the queen. He was sent to Asia Minor as viceroy about 407 B C; and after his father's death and the collapse of Athens he began to hire an army of his own, with a Greek mercenary corps that we know as the Ten Thousand. At last, in 401 B C, he began his long march to contest the throne with his elder brother, Artaxerxes II, and advanced unopposed to the vicinity of Babylon. There, by the Euphrates, on the battlefield of Cunaxa, he was confronted by the imperial army and was mortally wounded as he struggled to strike his brother down. Cunaxa was a pantomime battle. Suddenly abandoning his unstrategic retreat, the irresolute King had hurried forward against the invader, as though his only hope lay in joining battle before his commanders had time to change sides. The two armies stood facing each other in silence, waiting for Cyrus' Greek corps to strike. The Greeks advanced into missile range. Then, as they broke into their charge, the opposing Persian line turned round in flight and disappeared over the horizon with the Greeks in pursuit. Cyrus' followers were already making their salaams to him as King. But the presence of the river and the rules of Spartan infantry training had saved Artaxerxes; the Spartan in command of the Ten Thousand obstinately kept his unguarded right flank alongside the river, and the hammer-blow missed the Persian King. When the

Greek corps returned from its four-mile chase, Artaxerxes had already won the battle and was safely evacuating his unmounted forces from the field. The Greeks celebrated their victory, and only on the following day did they learn that Cyrus was not the victor. They thereupon offered the kingdom of Persia to the first comer, who with embarrassment declined it. Their casualty roll was one man hit by an arrow.

Fig. 39. Head of Tissaphernes on a satrapal silver stater, perhaps about 411 BC

Tissaphernes was left to deal with the Greeks. He had suffered an unnerving experience in the battle. His brigade, as Xenophon tells us, went into action against the Greek slingers; but the Greeks opened their ranks and made a lane down which the Persians galloped under fire from either flank. Tissaphernes himself came through this death-ride unhurt; and his exploit enabled him to overrun Cyrus' camp and be the hero of the day. But he could never again look Greek troops in the face; and it was the misfortune of this loyal satrap that, until he was executed for military incapacity six years later, he was continuously engaged in a hopeless struggle against a Greek army in Asia Minor. After Cunaxa, Tissaphernes had thought that he could break the spirit of the Ten Thousand by murdering their officers under cover of a truce. But this act of treachery only strengthened Greek morale. Tissaphernes then returned to Sardis and tried to annex the Greek cities. But after Cyrus' death the Spartans were in two minds about their treaty obligations to Persia. The Ten Thousand in the meantime fought their way through the snows of Armenia, and after a 2,000-mile march with their women and light baggage they reached the Black Sea at Trebizond. Their return was decisive; for here was a veteran corps ready for service in a Spartan expeditionary force. An army was formed, and under able leadership it ranged more and more boldly about western Asia Minor until Agesilaus was ready in 394 BC to carry the war into the eastern satrapies. But by this time Artaxerxes had seen the danger to his throne and he had commissioned a new fleet under a former Athenian admiral. Lavish bribes were now distributed to the enemies of Sparta in the Greek states and the resulting emergency at home led to Agesilaus' recall. A second mission in 391–90 came to grief through bad leadership, and the Spartans were so disillusioned that their government was thankful when in 386 BC it could force the Greek states to accept a peace dictated by Artaxerxes.

This peace – the 'King's Peace' – made over Cyprus and the cities of Asia to Persian rule. But Artaxerxes had little control over his western dominions, and the Eastern Greek world entered upon an uneasy phase of petty despotisms in the Aegean, with miniature empires on the Black Sea coast. The revolt of the satraps in the 360's again threatened the Persian empire with dissolution. But their rivalries impeded their common action; and, after Artaxerxes II's death in 358, Ochus began painfully to restore the central Persian authority until by the 340's the empire had recovered a certain degree of initiative.

THE NEW
URBANISM

The general insecurity in the first half of the fourth century had one advantage for the Eastern Greek communities. Cities and little despotisms had to look to their own protection, and consequently we find a revival of urban civilisation. Traces of new housing quarters of the early fourth century have come to light at Smyrna and Colophon, and an inscription of Erythrae testifies to a new lay-out with a comprehensive street system in the middle of the century; the new city of Priene was also laid out at that time, and we have some well preserved fortifications of this era in regular dry masonry – notably those of Assos where a banker set up his pacific rule. The town houses of these new fourth-century settlements were of poor construction; and by contrast with the well-built ones of a couple of hundred years earlier they have an air of impoverishment. But they were more convenient. The rooms made up in number for what they may have lacked in size. The roofs, being now tiled, did not require frequent attention. Domestic lavatories were by this

Plates 39, 40

time coming into fashion. A decrease in the size of bath-tubs no doubt meant less water to be fetched and heated; the sinking of wells in yards and open spaces saved a long carry with water jars, and the introduction of the hopper quern greatly eased the labour of grinding corn. These changes imply a more general change in the way of life. It is as though the fourth-century Ionians formed a 'middle class' – or rather a one-class society – which had little cheap labour at its disposal and regarded the convenient running of the house as a matter of prime importance. In cooking also a minor revolution had taken place. The old stock-pots, which simmered all day over the ashes, had been replaced by small, quick-heating cooking pots and tight-lidded stewpans.

The change to urban life is most clearly visible in regions where regular urban concentrations did not exist before, because in these circumstances completely new cities had to be laid out. The best examples in Eastern Greece are afforded by the Dorian cities and the neighbouring coasts of Caria. After the collapse of the Athenian empire, the three 'old cities' of Rhodes in 408 B C agreed to amalgamate and build themselves one great modern city. They appropriated for this purpose the triangular northern tip of their island and enclosed an area of about a square mile in a new fortification. On the more sheltered eastern side of the cape three bays were turned into a row of capacious harbours; and the ridge on the west side was made to serve as an acropolis. On the long, gentle slope in between, a regular chequer pattern of streets was laid out on an east-west axis. In the light of recent Greek investigations the ordinary streets seem to have been 10 feet in width; but every sixth one was a main street 14 feet wide, and on the transverse axis there is evidence for a boulevard 30 feet across, which was probably a distinctive feature of the original design. The three old cities of Rhodes continued to exist as subordinate townships; but the new city was the political centre. The union

Fig. 40

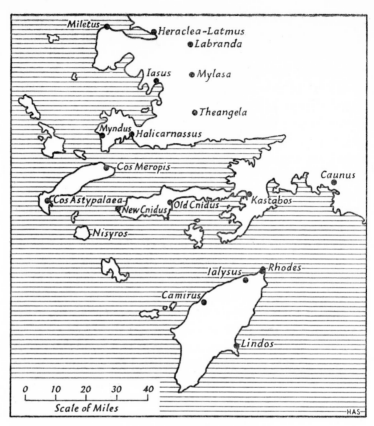

Fig. 40. The South-eastern Aegean in the fourth century BC

Fig. 44

set Rhodes on the highroad of history; and in the course of the next two centuries she became the greatest naval power in the world.

The other Dorian cities of this corner of the Aegean in due course followed the example of Rhodes. We learn from the ancient writers that in 366 the people of Cos transplanted their city to Meropis at the east end of their island; and archaeo-logical examination has revealed that perhaps about this time, but more probably a generation later, the Cnidians also removed to the tip of their promontory. In the fifth century the points of Cos, Rhodes and Cnidus had been mere capes to be rounded by ships plying between the Aegean and the Levant; but now they were occupied by new Dorian cities in magnificent commercial and strategical situations.

The city of Cnidus was probably the last of the three to be built, and it certainly had the grandest situation. It is worth pausing a little to consider its lay-out. Off the tip of the long, rugged peninsula, a rocky island lay broadside-on to the mainland. It only required an earth mole to join the two, and the strait was converted into a pair of excellent harbours. The smaller one, on the north-west of the isthmus, was reserved for the naval arsenal; it had stations for 20 warships; and narrowed by an artificial bulwark, its entrance could be closed with a chain. This harbour mouth was, so to speak, a gate in the city defences and was protected by towers. Southward from this, the circuit wall mounted obliquely above a gully to the cliff at the back; and the greater part of the former island was thus enclosed in the city defences. On the landward side, northeastward from the little harbour, the wall climbed along the edge of an arête to the mountain crest, at the far end of which a citadel 933 feet above sea-level formed the eastern redoubt of the city circuit. In the characteristic fashion of fourth-century military engineering the citadel wall on this height descends the topmost shoulders of the crest in pointed salients which would deny the enemy level ground for an assault on the curtain wall. From this citadel the circuit dropped sharply south-west to the sea.

The large south-east harbour was open to commerce. It connected with the naval harbour by a bridged canal and was itself sheltered by moles. The mole on the west side still stands clear in 16 fathoms of water. The eastern mole, however, has been submerged by the rise in sea-level; and though mentioned

CNIDUS

Plate 41

Plate 42

Fig. 41

Fig. 41. City wall and commercial harbour of Cnidus, with the 'island' beyond. View from the east. (After Krischen)

as a reef in the medieval Greek sailor's guide, it has escaped the notice of the *Mediterranean Pilot,* with the result that to the present day caïques riding low in the water strike on it when they put in to the deserted harbour under stress of weather. It might go ill with a master who followed the *Pilot's* advice that a ship may be laid on the beach there to prevent it from sinking.

In ancient times there was a residential quarter on the island, with houses built on parallel terraces. But the main inhabited area was on the mainland side, where a chequerboard plan of 'insulae' (blocks) measuring 175 by 100 feet was laid out in successive terraces on the slope. The uniformity of this housing scheme again seems to suggest a predominantly one-class society; and at Cnidus there is reason for believing that the democracy was established immediately after 334 B C, which is most probably the time when this new city was built. The temples and market buildings were mainly at the west end above the harbour heads; porticoes (stoas) were built by Sostratus, an architect of Cnidus who gained celebrity as the designer of the 440-foot-high lighthouse of Alexandria (the Pharos). Some-where in this vicinity, in its own special shrine, stood the nude Aphrodite (Venus) which the Cnidians bought from the sculptor Praxiteles after the people of Cos, with an excess of prudence, had taken a decently draped one instead. Ships passing up the coast into the Aegean must often have put in to Cnidus while waiting for the summer northerly to abate and allow them to round the cape; and the famous statue thus had many visitors. But pilgrims also came from a distance specially to see it. In front of the shrine was a garden with aromatic shrubs and arbours where the populace could enjoy their picnics. And in later times, at least, the shrine had a back door by which the caretaker would admit visitors who wished to admire the rear view of the goddess. The statue was so highly esteemed that a king of Bithynia offered to redeem the whole public debt of Cnidus in exchange for it.

The old town of Cnidus, which has only recently been recognised as such, lay a good day's walk to the east of the cape. Some of the agricultural population must have stayed on there after the removal, and consequently the old sanctuaries could not be transferred *in toto* to the new site. The new city therefore required a complement of new cults of the deities, who (like new citizens) could be granted admittance by the board of magistrates. It likewise required new images of the deities, of which Praxiteles' Aphrodite was no doubt one. The Aphro-dite herself has vanished, and the copies that survive can hardly do justice to the subtlety of the original. But in a precinct at the foot of a cliff Sir Charles Newton 100 years ago unearthed a fourth-century cult image, which he transported to the British Museum. This marble statue portrays Demeter. The

Plate 43

goddess is shown sitting, exhausted no doubt by her vain search for her daughter Persephone. She is a Mater Dolorosa; and, to bring out the pathos, the fourth-century artist has directed attention to the sad expression of the goddess' countenance by guiding the viewer's eye upwards from a confused tangle of drapery on which it cannot rest.

Above the houses at Cnidus was a building pointed out in later times as the observatory of Eudoxus, from which the famous Cnidian mathematician was said to have observed the star afterwards named Canopus. Above the houses also was a great theatre cut in the steep mountainside. And on the waterfront below there was a small theatre or concert hall where visiting artistes could give performances. Strabo tells us a story which illustrates the routine of daily life in one of the smaller cities of this corner of the Aegean. Fishing was the chief industry at Iasus, and a bell used to be rung at the time when the market opened. One day an itinerant harpist was giving a performance when the bell rang and his audience all walked out except for one man. Finishing his recital, the musician approached this man and congratulated him on his appreciation of music, for he alone of all the audience had not been lured away by the ringing of a bell. 'What's that you say?' shouted the deaf old man, 'Has the bell rung?'; and, muttering Adieu, he hurried off to inspect the day's catch.

Outside the city walls, of course, were the cemeteries. At Cnidus the rock was not soft enough to permit chambers to be cut, and many of the tombs were massive stone-built constructions with funerary altars set on a shelf over the entrance. Up the crest, sign-posted from the road, was the grave-precinct of a wealthy citizen called Antigonus, built in the early third century BC; it contained a race-track for the young men and a stand for musicians to play a piece from their repertoire to entertain the spirits of the dead man and his wife. Most of the tombs stretched in ribbon development along the roads, so that the dead might not be cut off from the traffic of the upper world or lack the occasional comfort of a pious tear; and along the main east road, which led up the peninsula, the tombs eventually extended for more than 3 miles from the city gate. In the countryside, the relics of massive stone terrace walls on the steep hillsides bear witness to intensive cultivation of the vines whose grapes yielded full-bodied wines for the Cnidian export trade. The traveller on this now unfrequented peninsula may observe traces of ancient buildings and sanctuaries, as also of the chain of forts that guarded the approaches to the city. The roads were feats of engineering and carried two lanes of traffic; and they played an important part in the economic exploitation of the Cnidians' land. Stone culverts were built to contain the streams, especially where they were spanned by wooden bridges. There still remains the greater part of a stone-built viaduct where the main route crossed a broader ravine; it carried a roadway 25 feet broad for a length of over 200 feet, with a triangular opening in the middle to let the torrent pass through. And six hours from the cape the foundations of an ancient inn may still be seen on top of a mountain pass where the traveller would rest after his laborious climb.

Plate 47

The new city of Cnidus was almost devoid of running water and it lay two hours' walk from the nearest arable land. We should therefore be justified in concluding that its foundation belongs to an era when commerce was taking first place in Eastern Greece; for otherwise the citizens would not have been willing to live under such inconvenience and so far from their fields. Once established, the new cities of this sort prospered for some hundreds of years until eventually the decay of commerce or Arab incursions drove the surviving inhabitants back to more primitive ways of life. It was not in the old Greek lands only that this new pattern of civic life was adopted in the fourth century BC. The barbarian tribes on the fringes of the Greek world were also being drawn inside the orbit of Greek

SPREAD OF
GREEK
CIVILISATION

civilisation. One of the most interesting instances of such a process is becoming known through Russian excavations in the Crimean region. Here a half-breed dynasty, the Spartocids, built up the so-called Bosporan Kingdom with its capital at Panticapaeum. In this new realm, into which many Scythian and Sarmatian tribesmen were absorbed, an industrial state with satellite towns came to life. Agricultural products and wine were processed; fish was cured, and the towns had their bronze-foundries, jewellers' workshops and manufactures of pottery and tiles. Another striking example is now for the first time being revealed by Bulgarian archaeologists. This is in some ways the more surprising because the excavations show that before the end of the fourth century the royal capital of the independent Thracians, Seuthopolis, was laid out in Greek fashion in the heart of Thrace many days' march from the sea.

In the next chapter we shall see how Alexander the Great and his Successors spread Greek civilisation in an Oriental world that they conquered by force of arms. From this tre-mendous movement of 'hellenisation' the era that they in-augurated has been named the 'Hellenistic Age'. But the hellenisation that took place in the generations before Alexan-der was in some ways more remarkable; for it was a purely spontaneous growth and not the result of conquest. Macedonia itself was being absorbed in the Greek world at the same time as it built up its military power. Greek culture was already penetrating high society in the Phoenician cities in the fourth century; cities of Asia Minor, like Sardis and the coastal towns of Pamphylia and Cilicia, were ready to emerge as Greek cities when Alexander liberated them, and the turn of savage Bithynia was soon to come. But the most systematic programme of hellenisation was that introduced by the Carian satrap Mausolus in his primitive country. Isocrates, an Athe-nian pamphleteer not lacking in political insight, was pro-claiming that the mark of the Greek was not race but participa-

MAUSOLUS
OF CARIA

tion in the Greek training for life. Mausolus recognised the significance of this for his own people: if the Carians were to play a part in the new world, they must adopt Greek city life, together with Greek institutions and language. His Carians were primarily a race of herdsmen living in little mountain-top towns. Mausolus compelled them to leave their old settlements, and concentrated them in new cities of up-to-date Greek design, which he equipped with the amenities of Greek political and social life. He even seems to have built a chain of police posts on the hill-top sites for fear that the people would lapse back into their old habits. But popular antipathy to the change was not long-lived. Within a generation or so these new cities took their place in the Greek world; and in the event there were no prouder guardians of the Greek heritage than they. The city of Caunus on the Lycian frontier was presently invited to send judges, in accordance with normal Greek practice, to arbitrate outstanding civil disputes at Smyrna. After the commission had completed its task, the people of Smyrna expressed their thanks in the usual way, and there the matter would have rested. But the Caunians were not inclined to let such an opportunity slip. They initiated a further exchange of compliments; and the long record of these transactions, engraved on stone and set up in public, stood ever after as a flatulent reminder of Caunus' new standing in the Greek world.

Plates 3, 4

These mushroom cities were most jealous of their dignity. Stratonicus, eminent alike as a harpist and a humorist, chanced to visit Caunus; and noting that the inhabitants were green in the face with marsh fever, he cried out, 'Ah! Now I understand what Homer had in mind when he said "As is the generation of leaves, even so is that of men".' When the Caunians expostulated that their city was insulted by being called unhealthy, 'But no!' replied Stratonicus, 'How could I call a place unhealthy where the very corpses walk in the streets?' Inevitably jokes were cracked about these parvenu cities. But they quickly made good. Caunus itself soon produced a famous painter and a successful administrator of a great estate in Ptolemaic Egypt; the Venus de Milo and the Farnese Bull bear the signatures of sculptors from other Carian cities; and in later times these little places were regularly represented by their bishops at the oecumenical Councils of the Church.

Mausolus and his successors had first-class Greek architects in their employment; and the results of their labours can still be seen in the fortifications of cities like Myndus, Heraclea-Latmus and Theangela, in the terraced complexes of the Carian sanctuary of Zeus at Labranda, and perhaps also in the initial lay-out of the new city of Priene (below, pp. 181–86). But the pride of Mausolus' architectural designing was Hali-carnassus, where he established his capital about 367 BC.

Fig. 42

Bearing a shrine of Apollo on its crest, the 'island' (where the Knights of St John founded the castle of St Peter in AD 1400) sheltered the harbour on the east side, and the spit of Salmacis closed it on the west. The palace of Mausolus, of brick and Proconnesian marble, lay in the vicinity of the 'island'. The city, enclosed in its great wall-circuit, was likened by an ancient writer to a theatre, with a boulevard running along the slope like a theatrical gangway. The adjoining drawing shows the lay-out diagrammatically as seen from up the slope. The Agora was by the waterfront. We know nothing of its arrangement except that a portico was built in the third century with aid from the king of Ptolemaic Egypt. But none of these public buildings rivalled the splendour of the adjacent pile (the Mauso-leum) which was built as the funerary temple of Mausolus and his family. The Mausoleum is said to have had 36 outer columns, while the chariot group that crowned the apex of the pyramidal roof stood 140 feet above the ground. It ranked as one of the Seven Wonders of the World. Statuary and sculptured friezes, which the ancient authorities attributed to great masters of the mid fourth century, decorated the exterior

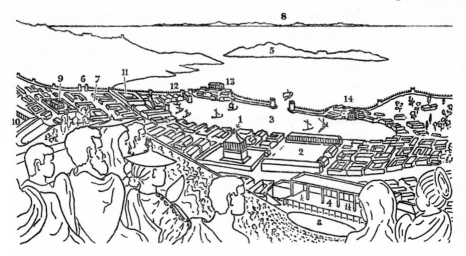

Fig. 42. Imaginative view of Halicarnassus in Hellenistic times, seen from above the theatre. 1, Mausoleum; 2, Agora; 3, Main harbour; 4, Theatre; 5, Arkonnesos Island; 6, Mylasa Gate; 7, Boulevard; 8, Cnidian Peninsula; 9, Demeter; 10, Gymnasium; 11 Palace; 12, Arsenal; 13, 'island'; 14, Salmacis

of the building; what survives of them is now in the British Museum. Effigies of Mausolus and his sister-consort Artemisia may have stood in the chariot on top of the roof; and if so, it is probably this very statue of the enlightened dynast that now faces the incoming visitor at the end of the south gallery in the British Museum – the unusual boldness with which the figure is carved seems to demand a position far from the viewer's eye.

Plate 44

When her husband died in 353 BC Artemisia is said to have pined away, but not before she had achieved fame by a memorable stratagem. The island of Rhodes had been subjected by Mausolus. But the story goes that after his death the Rhodians were properly contemptuous of a woman's rule and despatched a fleet to take Halicarnassus by surprise. The Rhodians sailed straight into the harbour and disembarked to capture the city.

But Artemisia was not prepared to submit. Her husband had built a concealed arsenal in the east corner of the harbour (a forerunner of the walled 'Box' harbour of Alexandria and the 'Mug' at Carthage). Here she secretly manned her warships and opened a canal to the bay behind the 'island'; and her sailors thereupon rowed round unexpectedly into the main harbour and towed away the enemy ships. Artemisia then manned the Rhodian ships with her own marines and sailed boldly for Rhodes; the unsuspecting Rhodians admitted their returning fleet, and the city was recaptured. Artemisia set up a victory monument in Rhodes; being dedicated to the gods, it could not be dismantled when the Rhodians recovered their freedom; so a high wall was built round it to conceal it from public view.

Until now our interest has centred mainly on particular peoples in the Eastern Greek world – Dorians, Aeolians and Ionians, together with their immediate neighbours; and these different peoples have been seen to possess distinct characters of their own. But in the fourth century such idiosyncracies were disappearing. In art, Phidias and the Parthenon had set their seal on a common Greek style. Architecture was losing its local peculiarities; and public buildings assumed more or less stereotyped functional forms. After Athens adopted the Ionic alphabet in 403 BC, a common system of writing became universal; and in due course Alexander's conquests led to a standardisation of spoken Greek (the 'Koine'). A similar trend towards uniformity was beginning to appear in the legal and constitutional procedure of the Greek cities and in the application of international law; and local and alien deities were absorbed with equality of status in the Greek pantheon, so that Homer's divine family was superseded by an ever-expanding republic of gods. The new archaeological evidence that has been brought into play in this chapter shows that in the fourth century this

increasingly homogeneous civilisation was no longer confined
to people of Greek blood but was already spreading to barbarians who cared to embrace Greek culture. With the conquests of Alexander the Great the process was extended across
the Persian Empire, so that the Greek world came to consist of
the sum of all the communities that embraced the forms and
institutions of Greek city life. In the remaining chapters we shall
therefore have in view a much larger and more heterogeneous
world comprising the Greek East, but one which was nevertheless united by a closer texture of common values and standards than had ever previously prevailed.

CHAPTER XII

Alexander and the Oriental World

IN THE SPRING of 334 BC, the young Alexander of Macedon began the great adventure of his short life by crossing
the Dardanelles into Asia. He had with him an army of less
than 40,000 men, a battle-fleet too weak to escort him past
Ionia, and a bare week's wages in his war-chest. He took some
Greek contingents with him, but they were mostly present as
hostages for the behaviour of the 'allied' states that he was
leaving behind him; the bulk of his combat troops consisted
of the Macedonians whom his father had converted into an
invincible fighting force. His intention was to conquer the
Persian Empire. Being small, his army was not greatly dependent on supply lines; Alexander thus enjoyed as great freedom
of movement as Cyrus had done, and he had one great advantage in the strength of his highly trained cavalry.

Fig. 43

Advancing inland, he defeated the satraps on the River
Granicus and marched south to Sardis and the Ionic coast.
Where he conquered the King's land he claimed it as his own.
But he gained the co-operation of the Greek cities by declaring
them free and exempting their land from tribute; and, contrary
to the Macedonian practice in Greece, he replaced the pro-
Persian rulers by democracies. Miletus offered a brief resistance.
But Alexander's most serious obstacle was Halicarnassus; for
the satrap's garrison there was strengthened by a Greek mercenary force, and it was inspired by the presence of Memnon of
Rhodes, to whom Darius III had entrusted the supreme command in the west. Alexander camped half a mile from the
Mylasa gate, and pending the arrival of his siege-train he made
an unsuccessful diversion to Myndus. He then set to work to
batter the eastern defences of Halicarnassus and at last succeeded in breaching the wall; but before he could force his way

in, the defenders ran up an inner curtain-wall of brick and held him out. After another indecisive battle the defenders sallied out in force, and Alexander's ambitions were almost extinguished; for he himself was defeated and disaster was only averted by his father's veterans in reserve. But by this time the defenders had suffered heavy losses; and garrisoning the strong points of Salmacis and the 'island', they abandoned the town to destruction at the hands of the Macedonians. Victory at Halicarnassus was not even then complete; the garrison there held out for a year against a force of over 3,000 men that Alexander left behind. But the generous treatment of the Ionic cities had had its effect, and Persian counter-attacks in the Aegean thereafter had little effect. More lenient treatment of captured Greek mercenaries also helped to make Alexander's subsequent task easier; for as his military reputation grew and that of Darius declined, the Greek units lost their inclination to fight to the bitter end in the Persian cause. After Halicarnassus the most serious danger to the Macedonians' success was not so much a military defeat as the chance of an accident to the person of their leader; for one of the secrets of Alexander's amazing generalship was his disregard for his own safety.

Alexander did not lay up his troops for the winter but spent the season in Lycia, where the snows prevented the natives from taking to the mountains. Then he traversed Asia Minor by a circuitous route, receiving a token submission from the Paphlagonians in the north and liberating or subduing the cities of the south coast. Darius had meanwhile made Damascus his headquarters; and as Alexander was pressing on into Syria in the autumn of 333, the Persian army cut his line of communications at Issus. The ensuing battle was decided by Darius' flight when his centre came under pressure. Alexander then made what for him was a bold decision. Instead of pressing home his advantage before Darius could summon fresh armies, he went south into Phoenicia and robbed the Persians

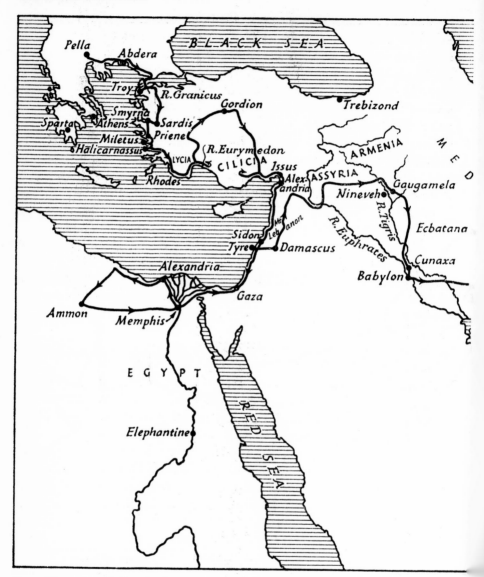

Fig. 43 The conquests of Alexander the Great

CASPIAN SEA

R. Oxus

R. Jaxartes

Maracanda

Alexandria
Eschate (Furthest)

SOGDIANA

Alexandria

BACTRIA

Alexandria
(Merv)

Bactra

HINDU KUSH

Alexandria

GANDHARA

Alexandropolis

Kabul

Bucephala

PARTHIA

Alexandria

R. Indus

R. Jhelum

Caspian
Gates

Alexandria

ARACHOSIA

Alexandria
(Kandahar)

Alexandria

Susa

Alexandria
Prophthasia

ELAM

Alexandria

CARMANIA

Persepolis

GEDROSIA

Alexandria

Patala

PERSIA

Alexandria

Alexandria

PERSIAN GULF

0   500

Scale of Miles

of their fleet bases. The other Phoenician cities welcomed him; but the aggressive defence of the island-city of Tyre held him up for seven months. Then in the late autumn of 332 Alexander entered Egypt, where he was received as a king and god; and at the western edge of the Delta he traced the outlines of a new foundation, Alexandria by Egypt, which was quickly to become the biggest city of the Mediterranean world. The architect commissioned to design this Alexandria was infected with the new enthusiasm for grandiose projects; for he is said to have offered to carve the 6,600-foot mountain of Athos into a likeness of Alexander pouring a libation, with a city on either hand and a river running from the one to the other.

In the months after the Battle of Issus the war entered its most critical phase. In Greece, Sparta formed a centre of resistance; cities changed hands in the Aegean, and the seasoned general Antigonus was hard pressed to hold central Asia Minor against the reorganised land forces of the Persian West. But Alexander's confidence in his subordinates was justified. In 332 the Persian counter-offensive slackened. Then, with the western satrapies conquered and their affairs settled, Alexander was at last ready to strike eastward; and in the high summer of 331 he advanced into Mesopotamia. Darius in the meantime had assembled a new army with brigades of elephants and scythed cars; he had had many months to practise, and on Alexander's approach he levelled a battle-pitch at Gaugamela near Nineveh. Alexander accepted the challenge on his opponent's terms. But he evaded the hazards, and in the decisive battle his cavalry held out long enough on the wings to enable him to drive Darius off the field. He then proceeded to capture the Persian capitals, and thus became master of a treasure so great that when put in circulation it formed a substantial proportion of the world's resources of coined money and bullion.

It might have seemed that Alexander was by this time approaching the end of his crusade. But, with the vast Iranian

Plates 45, 46

lands still virtually untouched, he chose to conquer the Persian Empire to its furthest limits; and at Susa he was in fact only half-way between his home at Pella and the furthest point that he was to reach in his journeyings. From Persia he pressed on through the Median highlands and the Caspian Gates until he caught up with the dying King; then, after a southward loop of hundreds of miles, he crossed the Hindu Kush and Bactria in the summer of 329 and entered the prosperous border province of Sogdiana. By way of Samarkand (Maracanda) he at last reached the frontier on the Jaxartes; there he founded the city of Alexandria the Furthest, and with the help of an artillery barrage crossed the river to dispel the northern nomads who were lining the opposite bank. The year 328 was spent in quelling serious risings of the eastern Iranian barons and plant-ing more new cities. Then in 327 Alexander descended through Gandhara into the Punjab and defeated the gallant Plate 65*a* rajah Porus in a great battle on the Jhelum. He was desper-ately keen to head eastward down the Ganges until he reached the Ocean; and it might have been better for his own peace of mind if he could have done so, though he would no doubt have discovered that the Golden Peninsula lay beyond. But the limits of the Achaemenid empire had by this time been passed, and the Macedonians at last mutinied. Alexander then cam-paigned in the Punjab, founding cities and setting up protec-torates; and he sailed down the Indus and established an arsenal at Patala. From there, after reconnoitring the Indian Ocean, he sent his admiral to circumnavigate the coast and him-self trekked round by the southern desert, suffering the same privations as his rankers, until the army reached the Persian Gulf early in 324 BC. He then fixed his capital at Babylon and was preparing a naval expedition in the Indian Ocean when he took ill of a fever and died in the summer of 323.

The trouble with Alexander was that he could not relax. He had worn his soldiers to the limit of endurance in ten years of incessant campaigning, often without respite in winter. Life was so short. So much still remained to be done, and he was already 32. He had hoped to make the Iranian nobles equal partners with his Macedonians in empire; he drafted Iranian troops into his army and tried to invest his person with oriental pomp and ceremony. But the Macedonians could not share their leader's exalted notions; and on his return to Babylon nearly all the native satraps had to be removed. Historians will never weary of disputing what the great conqueror's ultimate intentions were and what he would have become if he had lived; and it may be that he was really a great idealist. But it does seem clear that in the last years his character changed greatly. His despotic ways gave rise to fear, and fear to disaffection; and peace under him must have seemed a more dangerous prospect than war.

Of Alexander's many projects the most lasting was his new cities. He is said to have founded 70 of them. The figure may be an exaggeration, and it is of course true that some of these Alexandrias had long existed as native towns. But the new cities were genuine colonies. Greeks were left as citizens, together with a few Macedonians; and they received a law-code and plots of settlers' land. Alexander's policy was continued on a grander scale by his successors in Asia; and these cities, with their mixed Greek and Oriental population, became the centres of a common civilisation, culture and economic system.

THE GREEK
EAST AFTER
ALEXANDER

Alexander's empire did not disintegrate on his death. His generals and army held the satrapies together, and for four years they recognised the notion of a single centralised authority. But Ptolemy had meanwhile made himself undisputed master of Egypt; and when the old regent Antipater died in 319, the fragmentation of the unified command was no longer to be denied. The rival Successors struggled with one another for the possession of territory and the support of the remnants of the grand army; and by 304 BC the five great Macedonians who were established as sovereign rulers in the dominions conquered by Alexander had assumed the title of Kings. Ptolemy had held off all attacks on Egypt and founded a dynasty that finally came to an end with Cleopatra 300 years later. In Western Asia, the veteran Antigonus was predominant, and the greater part of the selfperpetuating nomadic hosts that had been Alexander's army gave him their allegiance and looked to him for pay and opportunities of loot. But his aggressive designs brought the rival kings into alliance against him, and he was defeated and killed in 301 BC. Antigonus' flamboyant son Demetrius survived the battle; and his descendants ruled in Macedonia, but he himself ended a roving career in debauchery as a pensioner of Seleucus in Syria. Lysimachus, who ruled in Thrace, succeeded to much of Antigonus' realm and proceeded to add Macedonia itself to his dominion. But presently the tide of feeling turned against him, and in 281 BC he was overthrown by Seleucus. By this time Ptolemy I had been dead a couple of years, and Seleucus was left as the sole survivor of Alexander's generals. For a moment he stood as ruler of virtually all Alexander's empire in Europe and Asia, and the great realm might after all have been united. But in that moment Seleucus was struck down by an assassin; and faced with fresh struggles at home, his son Antiochus I was not able to consolidate the new conquests.

Plate 65b

The Successors had fought under Alexander; they were strong men propelled by a personal ambition that kept them vigorous to a great age. But now that they were all dead, there was no single warlord left to claim the whole inheritance. Thus, a fluctuating balance of power was at last achieved; and though bones of contention were not lacking, a more stable pattern emerged in the political division of the Hellenistic world. Europe and Asia thereafter held apart.

In Egypt the Ptolemies paid special attention to the economic

organisation of their land and its commerce, and they proceeded to amass great wealth from it. But they had acquired
Demetrius' fleet; and in addition to owning Cyprus, they were
able until 200 B C to hold the Levant as far north as the Lebanon or beyond, together with a little empire in the Aegean and
those coastal parts of southern Asia Minor which could
supply Egypt's vast timber needs. Egypt was only very super-
ficially hellenised by the early Ptolemies, and the subsequent
history of Greek rule there is one of increasing concessions to
the political and religious demands of the natives, to which the
Rosetta stone in the British Museum bears witness.

The island of Rhodes formed a sort of business partnership
with the Ptolemies. As an independent city, Rhodes gained the
applause of the Greek world by withstanding the grand fleet
and siege-engines of Demetrius in 305–04 B C and thus showing that a war fought merely as an end in itself could be as
ineffective as it was futile. In the third century Rhodes made her
own fleet a dominant force and concentrated on keeping the
seas clear of pirates.

Fig. 44

Alexander had never visited the northern coasts of Asia
Minor, and his generals made little impression there. The
principal Greek cities were large and prosperous; and for the
most part they were able, in conjunction with the native kingdoms, to resist incorporation in the Hellenistic monarchies.
Except for Rhodes, there were no greater independent cities
in the Eastern Greek world than Cyzicus, Heraclea Pontica,
Sinope, and (across the Bosporus) Byzantium. Of the three
native kingdoms here, Paphlagonia never became politically
strong. But Bithynia began at once to take an important place
in the Greek world under a line of active kings who built
coastal cities of Greek stamp, adopted Greek court and chan-
cery styles, and encouraged trade with the Aegean. And further
east, the Persian dynasty of Mithridates Ktistes in Pontus was
not far behind in assuming the royal title, though the greatest

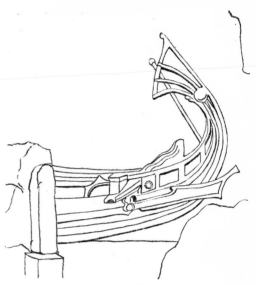

Fig. 44. Rock carving beside the stairway of the Acropolis of Lindos in Rhodes, representing the stern of a Rhodian warship (trihemiolia). The statue of its commander, Hagesander, was set up alongside. First half of the second century BC

era of this new kingdom only began after 183 BC when Pharnaces I captured Sinope by surprise and thus gained a place on the waterfront of the Hellenistic world. This group of powers formed a northern league in the early third century BC. They were united in resisting the Seleucid King of Syria, Antiochus I; and they secured their rear against him by planting a strong force of European Celts (the Galatians) on the Anatolian plateau.

Among those who deserted the cause of Lysimachus before his defeat in 281 was a man called Philetaerus who came from one of the Ionic colonies on the Black Sea. Philetaerus had been put in charge of the fortress of Pergamon, where a large part of the royal treasure was stored. On his death in 263 BC, his nephew Eumenes renounced his allegiance to the kings of Syria; and when Attalus I, who succeeded him in 241, won a victory against the pugnacious Galatians and assumed the royal title, a small kingdom came into being in western Asia Minor. Attalus was hard pressed for a time by the Seleucids.

Plate 65c

But when they gave up the attempt to capture Pergamon he set to work to enlarge his domains; and thanks to a prudent alliance with Rhodes and the expanding power of Rome, the new kingdom of Pergamon quickly became dominant in the western half of Asia Minor.

The main kingdom of the East was of course that of the Seleucids. Seleucus himself had been a late starter in the race for power. After recovering Babylon in 312 B C, he set to work to secure for himself the satrapies of the East. But it was only in 301 that he gained possession of Syria and made the Orontes valley the kernel of his empire; and, as we have seen, it was only at the very end of his life that he extended his realm across Asia Minor and became for a moment the greatest monarch of his age. He had wisely relinquished Alexander's *Fig. 45* Indian conquests to the new Mauryan emperor Chandragupta in return for a treaty of amity and 500 war elephants. But the Seleucid realm in Asia still extended across 45 degrees of longi-

Fig. 45. Terracotta figurine found at Myrina in Aeolis, now in the Louvre. Indian war elephant with rug, tower and bell, striking down a Galatian, perhaps in the campaign of Antiochus I of Syria

tude; and being interlopers in the eyes of the Iranian nobles and one of several contending dynasties in Greek eyes, the Seleucids could not command sufficient loyalty to keep both ends of their empire quiet at one time. Consequently they were incessantly struggling to maintain the *status quo*. In the West, the Ptolemies disputed their possession of the maritime fringes, the Galatians were disturbing the peace of central Asia Minor, and the Attalid Kingdom was expanding round Pergamon; and there were bigger developments in the East.

In the mid third century a nomadic people known in history as the Parthians gained possession of the region south-east of the Caspian and so drove a wedge into the middle of the Seleucid empire. The eastern provinces of the empire were thus isolated from the West. The region of southern Afghanistan (the ancient Arachosia) seems at this time to have come into Indian possession; for a rock-inscription found in 1958 at Kandahar -- the site presumably of an ancient Alexandria -- records the benefits of Aśoka's temperate rule in parallel Greek and Aramaic texts. We may thus infer that the region had been lost by the Seleucids before 250 BC; and from the lettering of the Greek text, which is by no means backward or provincial, we may deduce that full contact with the Greek world had been maintained in the preceding generations. To the north of this, in Bactria and Sogdiana, the Greek satrap held his own; he seems in fact to have made himself a quasi-independent ruler. A generation later a Greek of Magnesia named Euthydemus enlarged the boundaries of the principality; and when Antiochus the Great was reconquering the eastern satrapies near the end of the century, Euthydemus' stubborn defence earned him recognition as an independent monarch. Bactria thus became the centre of a powerful kingdom in which, in increasing isolation from the Mediterranean world, Greeks and Iranians co-existed in harmony. Euthydemus' son, Demetrius, carried on the work. He proceeded to invade India in the 180's;

Plate 65e

165

and helped by Buddhist sentiment, he created a Graeco-Indian realm whose far-flung principalities endured for 100 years after the parent Bactrian kingdom had itself collapsed. Greeks and Indians seem to have lived together as citizens; Indians held civic offices in the Greek cities; and Greek continued to be used, as a heraldic language at least, through a large part of the first century after Christ.

Excavation may some day throw a clearer light on this peculiar Indo-Greek civilisation. There is some ground for thinking that the setting for Indian drama may have been inspired by Greek plays or mimes – at least, the word for the backcloth of the later Indian stage was 'Yavanika' ('Ionic', i.e. Greek); improvements were probably introduced at this time in Indian medical practice, and at some stage also Greek astronomy was accepted in India. In art, however, the influence of the Hellenistic world seems to have been relatively slight; for it was only in Roman times, and with Parthia as the intermediary, that the sculptural style of Gandhara came into being under the impact of western forms. On their side, the Greeks seem to have been ready to embrace Buddhism as a religious philosophy and to learn Indian customs and language. In general, they considered the Indians to be among the 'best' barbarians. We may perhaps recapture something of their admiration for a way of life totally different from their own if we read through the text of Aśoka's inscription at Kandahar: 'After completing ten years of his reign King Piodasses (i.e. Aśoka) displayed Piety to mankind, and thereafter he made men more pious, and everything flourishes throughout the earth; and the King abstains from eating creatures that have life [the Aramaic version more correctly says that *little* meat is killed for his table], and the rest of mankind does likewise; and the King's hunters and fishermen have stopped hunting; and people who were intemperate before have given up their intemperance as far as they are able; and they are more obedient to their fathers and mothers and their elders, and by so doing they shall live better and more righteous lives henceforward.'

Antiochus III of Syria received the title of 'Great' because of   Plate 65*d*
his success in subduing the Parthians and reasserting Seleucid supremacy in the East. But he was less successful when he returned to the West. After their conquest of Carthage the Romans had become involved in the vicissitudes of Greek politics. The repute of Antiochus' power alarmed them; and allying themselves with his enemies, they inflicted a crushing defeat on him at Magnesia under Sipylus in 189 BC. In the ensuing treaty the Seleucids were deprived of all their territory in Asia Minor except for a foothold on the Cilician coast; despite the vigorous policies of Antiochus Epiphanes the loss of their eastern possessions followed, and the Parthians took possession of Babylonia and the upper course of the Tigris. Constant interference by Rome prevented any lasting recovery on the part of the Syrian kings. Their realm thus shrank to a mere principality on the Levant coast; Hellenism declined, and a Greek Orient, equal in extent to the whole western half of the Roman Empire, was lost to the Mediterranean world. Within a couple of hundred years of Alexander's conquests Manifest Destiny in the East ended in Evident Ruin beyond the Euphrates.

Considering the great extent of their power and the fact that they were to be the most dreaded enemy of Rome for several centuries, the Parthians are a strangely colourless people. They rose to power before the Greek world could assimilate them. But they acquired a smattering of Greek culture and institutions, and their court was evidently half-hellenised. The story was told that the Parthian King Orodes, in company with the   *Fig. 46*
visiting king of Armenia, was listening to a recitation of Euripides' *Bacchae* when unexpectedly the severed head of Crassus was brought in from the battlefield to enact the part of dismembered Pentheus. The Parthians did not destroy the

Fig. 46. Orodes I, King of Parthia about 55–37 BC, wearing diadem and torque, on a silver coin

Greek cities. In fact, the Greeks retained their language and customs, and the cities formed the centres of culture and econo‑ mic life in the new Oriental kingdoms that were carved out of the Seleucid domains. The most favoured winter residence of the Parthian court was at Ctesiphon only three miles from the old eastern capital of the Syrian kings, Seleucia on the Tigris; and the destruction of this Seleucia in AD 165 was not the work of the Parthians but of a Roman army which had been received with friendship by the Greek citizens. A portrait statue of a Parthian chieftain is reproduced in one of our plates. Other photographs show the mountain‑top burial sanctuary of the kings of Commagene – a principality on the upper Euphrates that broke away from the Seleucid empire before the middle of the second century BC.

Plate 48

Plates 49, 50

NEW CITIES With few exceptions, the new cities founded by Alexander and his Successors in the Orient had in the first instance been quasi‑military colonies guarding the routes and forming out‑ posts against the threat of attack. The original Greek settlers were mainly soldiers and veterans; and these towns, in so far as they have been explored, seem to present a rigid, almost barrack‑like appearance; no doubt a similar regularity would have been visible in the plots of settlers' land. Of course, many volunteers from the old Greek cities and from the hellenised lands came to these new foundations in the hope of a more promising future; and, in a few cases, cities like Miletus and Magnesia sent organised bodies of colonists to form the core of a new settlement. But in general the new cities were personal

foundations of the monarchs themselves. In North Syria the
great metropolitan centres of the Seleucids were Antioch and
Apamea in the Orontes valley, together with Seleucia and
Laodicea on the coast. Antioch became the civil capital here
and Apamea the military base. This region was the most
intensively hellenised in the whole Orient; and while the great
cities were named after kings and queens, a whole series of
place-names like Pella, Beroea and Pieria bore witness to the
Seleucids' intention of converting North Syria into a second
Macedonia. No doubt South Syria would have become equally
hellenised if it had come into the hands of the early Seleucid

Plate 51

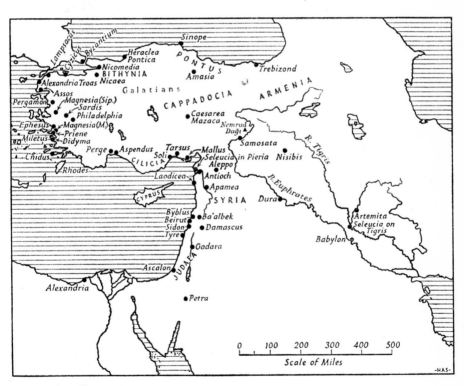

Fig. 47. The Hellenistic East

169

kings; but it was owned by the Ptolemies of Egypt, who were not hellenising city-builders. In early Hellenistic times the population of Antioch will have been less than the quarter-million or more inhabitants that lived there under the Roman empire; but the original city under Seleucus seems nevertheless to have been about a mile long and half a mile broad. The Mesopotamian region was not so densely studded with Greek settlements. But Seleucia on the Tigris, which supplanted Babylon and was itself succeeded by Baghdad, had a greater population even than Antioch.

In these capital cities the number of Greek immigrants engaged in agriculture, business and the civil services may quickly have run into five figures. On the other hand, the harbour town of Seleucia in Pieria, which had fallen into Ptolemaic hands, had no more than 6,000 adult male citizens a hundred years after it was founded; and there were smaller settlements on the caravan routes, like Dura (Europus) at the crossing of the Euphrates. To judge by the results of recent French research, these new foundations seem to have had certain common features. A citadel on a conveniently situated hill was designed to house the garrison. Below this lay the residential settlement, enclosed in a fortification that followed the contours of the ground. The town quarters were laid out on a severely regular chessboard plan, with streets more than 20 feet broad and residential blocks whose length was regularly double their breadth. One street seems normally to have been singled out as a broader boulevard. But the colonnaded avenues with roundabouts at the main crossing, such as may be seen at Gerasa, do not seem to have made their appearance until Roman times; and there was perhaps a lack of grand monumental buildings and handsome vistas in the Seleucid cities. Where existing towns were hellenised, as for instance at Damascus or Aleppo, a simple residential quarter on a chequerboard plan seems to have been built alongside the

Alexander and the Oriental World

native settlement, and the two were enclosed in a single fortification. Antioch too had its native quarter in the original city
plan; but it is said to have lain outside the fortified circuit.

In the lands which were already Greek there was of course
not the same need for new cities. But the policies of Alexander's
Successors demanded considerable changes. When the Greeks
of western Asia Minor were liberated by Alexander, numerous little cities celebrated their newly-won freedom by striking
their own bronze coins; and consequently the modern scholar
gains the impression that at that time there were more independent Greek cities in the world than ever before. But many of
these little places were too small to provide for their own defence
or continue to function as self-governing communities in the
new world of power politics; and the Successors wanted strong,
well-defended cities to act as focal points in their kingdoms.
Thus, for example, Antigonus created a new city of Antigonia,
later called Alexandria Troas, in which half a dozen old cities
of the Troad were merged; and after Antigonus had failed to
induce Teos and Lebedos to amalgamate, Lysimachus compelled the inhabitants of Colophon and Lebedos to remove to
a great new city that he founded at Ephesus. Force was sometimes needed to put these 'synoecisms' into effect. Not without
justice, the Colophonians refused to leave their old home until
Lysimachus sent troops and defeated them in battle; and we are
told that the Ephesians themselves would not abandon their
existing town until he blocked the culverts in a storm and so
flooded them out. But, once established, these strong cities
dictated the pattern of Hellenistic life. Country life seems
almost to have come to an end among the Greeks here. The
citizens had their homes in the city, from which presumably
they would go out to work in their fields at the appropriate
seasons. The remains of Hellenistic habitation that the archae-
ologist now finds in the countryside seem to belong almost
exclusively to garrison positions; and it was not until the Pax

Romana was firmly established in Imperial times that country life was resumed on any large scale. As we shall presently see, it was in the Hellenistic Age that the Greeks really became specialists in the art of city-dwelling.

The founding of new cities and amalgamation of old ones was in itself no small task. The first essential was fortifications; and we learn from an inscription of Colophon that when – probably on their return from exile after Lysimachus' fall in 281 BC – the citizens there subscribed from their own resources for the rebuilding of their city, the architect was engaged in the first instance to plan the wall-circuit. But an agora and a street system had also to be laid out, and building plots had to be divided up. Quarried stone, marble, metals and wood will usually have been needed in bulk, and brickyards and tile factories must be set in operation. Statues and furnishings were required for the sanctuaries. Surviving documents show that, in the case of completely new settlements, stock and seed-corn and farm implements were needed; and not only architects but skilled masons and technicians had to be found. The kings to some extent maintained teams of such specialists. They also had to assist the new foundations by remitting taxes and even by direct financial aid; and the phrase that sometimes occurs in the documentary inscriptions, of the King personally 'taking forethought' for the new settlement, implies the need of a dynamic driving force in the background. These new cities were not just a matter of a blueprint and a royal fiat; each one demanded effort and attention, as well as financial outlay, on the part of the ruler who founded it. In Chapter XIV we shall consider more closely how the Hellenistic city functioned. But first we may pause to survey the progress that the Greeks were making in their acquaintance with the outer world.

CHAPTER XIII

From the Arctic Ocean to the China Sea

O RIGINAL THOUGHT and scientific discovery survived the age of Plato; and at the beginning of the Hellenistic era there were Greek thinkers equal to the giants of the past. Indeed, in many directions the third century was the climax of Greek thought, when Strato of Lampsacus experimented to prove fundamental physical theories and Aristarchus of Samos maintained against heavy odds that the earth rotates on its axis and revolves round the sun. Considerable progress was made in engineering also, though the Hellenistic Age was no exception to the general rule that in the ancient world such advances were closely connected with spectacular royal or imperial projects and with military emergencies. But the attitude towards learning was changed. What in effect had happened was that the new Hellenistic East offered unlimited possibilities to men of ability and education as administrators, high officials and professional men; and a large proportion of the abler and more enterprising Greeks found full-time occupations of this sort in the new kingdoms. As the new specialisation created its professionals, thought became professionalised too; the pursuit of knowledge developed into academic learning, and learning into scholarship. Early in the third century the Ptolemies founded an institute of advanced study at Alexandria; and at this centre, which was called the 'Museum', a library of half a million volumes was formed. Gradually the scholars who assembled at this and other academies turned their minds to collecting, studying and imitating the writings of past generations – in fact, to the study of the Classics; and the era of creative genius slowly gave way to that of critics, compilers and commentators. This does not mean that people were becoming less educated. The general level of education was rising. The

Classics were studied by educated natives in the new kingdoms; and it is to the devoted labours of the great Hellenistic scholars that we owe the fact that our western heritage of militant Christianity has been so providentially mitigated by classical humanism.

Among the greatest brains of the Museum in the third century was Eratosthenes of Cyrene, who was called 'Beta' (or 'Number 2') because he was regarded as the runnerup in each of the various branches of intellectual activity. It had been recognised for some time that the earth is a sphere; and Eratosthenes calculated its size correctly and plotted the positions of the known continents. It thus became clear that the known world could only occupy a small part of the total surface of the globe; and it was suggested that there must be other great landmasses to correspond to that of Europe, Asia and Libya combined. If later scholars had not perverted Eratosthenes' calculations and halved the estimate of the intervening space, Columbus would have entertained little hope of reaching India by sailing west.

Fig. 48

The reconstruction of Eratosthenes' map serves to show what enormous advances the Greeks had made in their acquaintance with the world. Knowledge of the northwest of Europe came from a hardy Ionic captain of Massalia, named Pytheas, who slipped through Carthaginian waters to prospect the tin trade about the time when Alexander was penetrating the Further East. He brought back word of Britain and islands beyond; and he probably encountered Arctic fog, for he claimed that he only abandoned his voyage beyond Thule when sky, sea and land all merged into one. Pytheas plotted his latitudes accurately. But he could only estimate longitude by guessing the speed at which he was sailing; and as he overestimated the length of Britain, the island had to be slewed round on the maps to enable its estimated length to fit within its range of latitude. Eratosthenes accepted these discoveries;

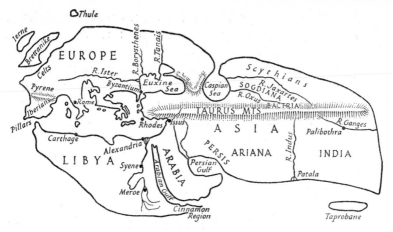

Fig. 48. Eratosthenes' Map of the World, third century BC. *(After various modern reconstructions.) Eratosthenes gave the circumference of the earth at the equator as 250,000 stades (25,000 miles or more), and he seems to have calculated the length of Europe and Asia combined as about 70,000 stades. We learn from the geographer Strabo that his axis was a parallel running from the Pillars of Heracles (i.e. the Straits of Gibraltar) through Rhodes and Issus and along the foot of the Taurus range to Mt Imaion (Himalaya). Other parallels are mentioned, together with meridians; and sufficient distances are given to make the reconstruction of his map tolerably accurate*

but they were not followed up, and later generations affected to regard Pytheas as an impostor.

Accurate knowledge of the Indian Ocean was late in coming. Admittedly, Alexander's staff had made detailed notes, especially of their overland routes. But Eratosthenes' fresh data came only from Greek officials and ambassadors who could not have travelled far off the main routes, and from hearsay obtained through traders. The 'Cinnamon Coast' of Somaliland was of course familiar to merchants of Ptolemaic Egypt; and luxury goods were entering the Seleucid Kingdom by caravan routes from the Further East or coming to Egypt through Arab middlemen. But the secrets were jealously guarded, and little was known of the sources of this traffic. It was not until the late second century BC that Greek merchant seamen made direct contact with India; and even then it was the result of a chance encounter. The following story, which accounts for the beginning of Greek voyaging to the East, was related by Posidonius as having happened when he was a young man; it may be unreliable in some details, and Strabo refused to believe in it; but Strabo was equally sceptical about Pytheas and other reliable authorities, and Posidonius can hardly have invented such a story.

About 120 BC the Egyptian Red Sea guards brought in an Indian who had been found half-dead on a drifting ship. King Ptolemy VIII had him taught Greek, and the man then offered to act as a guide to the Indian coast. A citizen of Ionic Cyzicus, called Eudoxus, happened to have come to Alex-andria on a mission and was sight-seeing in Egypt at the time; he volunteered to make the journey and in due course returned with a valuable cargo of spices and jewels. In fact he made two voyages, but each time he was obliged to surrender his cargo to the king. On the second voyage, however, the monsoon must have carried him far down the East African coast. He compiled a vocabulary of the language spoken there, and he picked up a ship's figurehead which was duly identified as belonging to a fishing smack of Cadiz. Eudoxus thereupon concluded that it was possible to circumnavigate Africa and circumvent the avaricious rulers of Egypt. He returned home; and selling his property, he fitted out an expedition, taking with him doctors and craftsmen, as well as cabaret-girls for the Indian princes. Sailing out into the Atlantic, they ran into trouble on the West African coast. But Eudoxus got safely back; and now he was quite certain that Africa could be rounded, because on this journey he had reached a point where people spoke the lan-guage he had previously studied. So he fitted out a second expedition; and this time he took on board joiners, farm imple-

ments and seed-corn so that the party could halt and grow crops
en route. No one knows whether he rounded the Cape or was
the first captain to reach India by the long sea passage; like the
Vivaldi Brothers, who attempted the same feat in the year 1291,
he was not heard of again.

These explorers had courage; for they had neither fire-arms to
cow the natives nor fire-water to corrupt them. No Greek, so
far as we know, ever attempted to follow in Eudoxus' track
round the Cape. But his shorter crossing from the Red Sea
quickly became a well-explored route once the Greek sailors
learned to take advantage of the summer monsoon. At first the
crossing was to the Indus mouth, and Patala flourished as the
centre of the East Indies trade. But before long the seamen
learned to steer for more southerly ports, straight for the heart
of the South Indian pepper country. Evidently this had already
become normal before the Roman conquest of Egypt; for cave-
inscriptions show that Indo-Greek merchants from the Greek
cities of the Indus valley were doing business down at Bombay
soon after 50 BC; and, only a generation or so later, Graeco-
Roman domestic pottery was being used at Pondicherry
(Poduce), where an old fishing village had sprung to new life
as the emporium for cross-country trade to the Malabar coast.
The journey from the Red Sea was quick, though not without
danger from storms and pirates. Standing out to sea off the horn
of Africa (Cape Gardafui), the big merchantmen ran with the
wind on their quarter to Broach or the Malabar coast within
40 days. They carried choristers, girls for the rajahs' harems,
metals, clothing, sashes and ointment, together with gold and
silver coin for currency. But what the Indian poet especially
recommended was the cool, fragrant wines brought in these
beautiful Yavana ships that made the water white with foam.
In Indian ports the Greeks loaded pepper and spices, jewels,
silk and cotton cloth, ivory, cosmetics and other luxuries; and
they returned with the midwinter monsoon.

As the demand for exotic products increased, Roman capital must have been invested in the trade. Whole fleets would sail with the monsoon; and a sailor's handbook was published so that skippers who were new to these waters would know what trade was carried on at different ports, or where pilots could be picked up and what western goods the Arab sheikhs liked best. Yavana (Greek) merchants came to settle in Indian ports. Native princes employed Yavana bodyguards, and Yavana engineers were in demand. The Yavanas must have become a legend in later ages; for in the eleventh century of our era a Kashmir poet could credit them with the ability to fly aeroplanes. This is the obverse side to Juvenal's sneering comment that the starveling Greek would go up to the sky if you told him to do so.

Compared with this brisk traffic on the Malabar coast, Greek commerce beyond the southern tip of India was relatively limited. But some Greek seamen did sail to the Coromandel coast and the Gulf of the Ganges and discover that the best pearls and muslin are to be had there; and the Far East was also visited. The last of the known voyages of fresh discovery, probably about the early second century after Christ, is attributed to a man who bore the appropriate name of Alexander. He may have been the first westerner to use the monsoon for making an open-sea crossing of the Bay of Bengal; and as he gave a description of the voyage to Cattigara, we must assume that he penetrated into the South China Sea and up the coast of Annam; he may have gone even further, but the precise position of Cattigara is not known. The first regular contact with the Chinese court, under the Han dynasty, is dated to AD 166 at a time when the interruption of the caravan trade across Asia had caused a serious silk shortage in the Roman Empire. The merchants, who crossed the Chinese frontier from Annam, were recorded as an embassy sent by An-tun (presumably the emperor Marcus Aurelius Antoninus); but the later Chinese chronicler, to whom we are indebted for our knowledge of the event, noted that the 'tribute' brought by these 'ambassadors' had contained no jewels and he rightly doubted their credentials. The direct silk trade which was then opened seems to have continued for a century or two; but little is known about it, and only very vague knowledge of Sumatra, Java and Borneo reached the western world. It may be that such Greek traders as operated in these seas were permanently resident in the Indies, because a voyage from Suez to China and back would have taken several years to accomplish.

CHAPTER XIV

City Life in the Hellenistic Age

IT IS COMMONLY ASSERTED by modern scholars that the Greek city came to an end with Alexander the Great and that the one worth-while political idea of the Hellenistic Age was monarchy. This judgement is of course prompted by the belief that Athens and the old Greek motherland were always the true focus of Greek political life; and in Hellenistic times the old motherland was in political decline with Athens becoming an old-fashioned university town. Again, the absence of violent constitutional changes in the Hellenistic cities might seem to imply political stagnation; for in earlier times the one sure sign of a vigorous city life was political instability. But these assumptions are not wholly valid. When we turn to the cities of the Eastern Greeks, the lack of serious dissension seems rather to be a sign that internal problems had been satisfactorily solved and that a healthy civic life had developed. Democratic constitutions had been sanctioned by Alexander. In principle, at least, the citizens were all equal; and well-to-do members of the community who were elected to public office were ready to shoulder civic burdens and distinguish themselves by generous benefactions. Likewise, the numerous interstate agreements, arbitrations, and exchanges of citizen rights, which are recorded in the inscriptions of the cities, are proof of a responsible attitude towards the conduct of external affairs. The individual cities had become less exclusive and more inclined to co-operate with one another.

As the Hellenistic world developed, the biggest cities in point of population were the capitals of the new kingdoms, which were under royal supervision. But the older cities of the Eastern Greeks had the longest traditions; and most of the greater ones retained the full sovereignty of their body-politic, together with a considerable degree of initiative in external affairs. Rhodes, Cyzicus, Byzantium, Heraclea Pontica and Sinope were independent powers; Smyrna and Miletus were virtually so; and in the main the cities of Eastern Greece enjoyed greater freedom than had been permitted them under Persian or Athenian rule. The political initiative of the cities may thus be said to have reached its climax in early Hellenistic times; and the statement that the history of the Greek city ended with Alexander appears to be little more than a corollary of the old belief that the serious study of Greek history as a whole ends with Alexander the Great.

In this chapter the evidence produced will be mainly archae-ological, the aim being to show the background against which civic life was lived in the Hellenistic Age; and more particu-larly, we shall be considering the first century and a half or two centuries of that age before political life succumbed to apathy and before the decline of originality led to the degradation of taste. In Chapter XII something was said about the planning of Seleucid cities in the East; and our account of the Hellenistic cities would be more complete if we could examine some of those great centres in closer detail. But the archaeology of the Seleucid empire is still in its infancy; and Dura – the one town where excavation has been carried to a successful conclusion – has yielded only a faint impression of the Hellenistic settlement. Consequently, the examples presented in this chapter are of necessity drawn from the better explored region of Western Asia Minor.

Our best specimen of a Hellenistic city is Priene, which lay opposite Miletus. Thanks to the German excavators its plan has been recovered almost entire and the appearance of many of its buildings is known. The new city at Priene was probably founded just before 350 BC under the name of Naulochon; and since the steeply sloping site was evidently chosen for the sake of the dominating 1,250-foot-high rock that formed the

PRIENE: ITS
LAY-OUT

Fig. 49

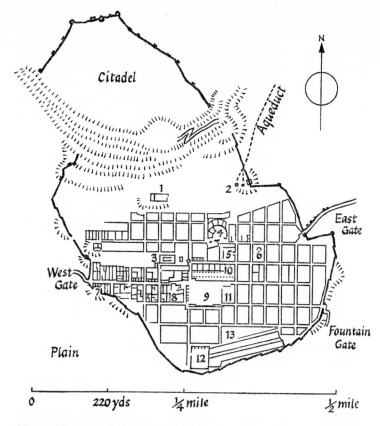

Fig. 49. Priene, ground-plan of site (after Kleiner). 1, Shrine of Demeter; 2, Reservoir tanks and basin; 3, Temple of Athena; 4, Theatre; 5, Upper Gymnasium; 6, Sanctuary of Egyptian Deities; 7, Sanctuary of Cybele; 8, Market; 9, Agora; 10, Council Chamber; 11, Sanctuary of Zeus and Asclepios; 12, Gymnasium; 13, Stadium

citadel, we may conjecture that the founder was a ruler who intended to maintain a garrison there – probably therefore the satrap of Caria. The city wall was carefully sited to take what advantage it could of the ground; and inside this circuit a town was laid out for perhaps 5,000 inhabitants. Though it had its harbours no great distance away, Priene remained always a country town. The temple of Athena, which was dedicated by Alexander the Great, was designed in the Ionic order by Mausolus' chief architect, Pytheos; set on a high terrace, with a colonnaded Doric stoa forming a screen along its side, this handsome building was the most conspicuous in the town. But it was its situation that made it a landmark. In scale it did not exceed the other public buildings; and it thus draws attention to the fact that religious buildings are not going to count for more than secular ones in the Hellenistic cities. Orthodox religion was passing into a decline.

Plate 53

The bulk of the buildings that appear in the German model are houses. They vary greatly in size and arrangement. Many had a narrow frontage and must have been cramped; but where there were only four houses to a building block, the dimensions were about 80 feet by 60, and this allowed room for a relatively large yard inside the house-plot, with the main apartments to the north and lesser rooms ranged along other sides. Generally, the main room had a vestibule or corridor in front of it; this served to trap the midday sunlight in summer, but did not prevent the low winter sun from penetrating further in. The roofs were of course tiled, and for the most part they probably had a single slope. It is not known whether the main part of the house was commonly two-storeyed. External windows were probably few, small, and set high in the wall. The walls of the rooms were plastered in imitation of marble; bronze bed fittings, terracotta braziers and marble tables came to light in the excavations. A new feature of the lay-out here was rows of small shops bordering main avenues.

Plate 53

Fig. 50

Before we turn to public buildings we may pause to observe the effect of a systematic city lay-out of this sort. The relationship of the parts to the whole is a conscious one. The heart of the city stands open for everyday life to proceed in full view. The buildings present no violent contrasts of grandeur and meanness; they have a quiet, well-proportioned dignity and seem to provide a uniform background against which man would have appeared in scale.

ITS CIVIC AMENITIES The architect of Priene was able to incorporate the recreational buildings inside the city-circuit. In the upper part of the town was the theatre, which probably held 5,000 spectators comfortably. The principal shows in Hellenistic times were given by the 'Artists of Dionysus', who formed travelling repertory companies, and whose visit was the occasion of a fête in each city; these players performed drama and variety and expected a good recompense, but they did on the odd occasion give their show gratis if a city exchequer was empty. In most of the cities the theatre was also used for other purposes, including assemblies of the citizens.

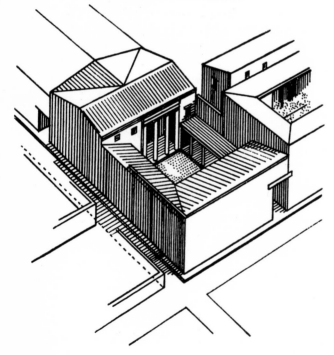

Fig. 50. Durm s restoration of a large house at Priene, seen from the south-west. The main suite with the columnar porch at the north end of the courtyard is usually restored with a gabled front

At the foot of the town of Priene was a group of buildings comprising a 'palaestra' (wrestling-ground) and stadium (race-track), together with dressing-rooms, wash-basins and other apartments; from the second century B C onward this was the chief gymnasium of Priene. As the old discipline of family life weakened, the gymnasium became the main training-ground for citizenship in the Greek cities; and the general educational system that it served was directed towards both physical and mental health. Every city had a gymnasium for its youths of what we might call school-leaving age; some also had separate gymnasia for boys and for young men, and occasionally even older men were provided for. The Hellenistic cities maintained a regular establishment of paid teachers and athletic trainers, and the public doctors played their part there. Prizes were awarded for good conduct, physical condition and hard work, as well as in set subjects of study. The office of head of the gymnasium was both an honourable and an onerous one. Sometimes a wealthy citizen gave an endowment to ease the burden; and others showed their patriotism by making dona-tions, especially of oil for athletics. Libraries were formed in the gymnasia, and music of course had a leading place. In later Hellenistic times, when city politics lost some of their attraction, the gymnasia became the most important centres of public life in the cities. Some of the teachers were devoted to their work, like Diotimus who distressed the poet Aratus by settling down in a backward town of the Troad:

> Alas, poor Diotimus!
> Upon the rocks sits he,
> Teaching the boys of Gargara
> To say their ABC.

The Agora, or principal public square, was lined with stoas and formed the centre of civic activity. It was incorporated in the city plan in such a way that no streets intersected it and the dignity of public intercourse was not disturbed by traffic. The provisions market, whose supervision was in the hands of special officials, was screened off by a stoa from the end of the Agora. The Agora contained monuments, altars and statues, which were not merely adornments but memorials of the history and cults of the city; and the adjacent stoas may have housed public offices. Just above the right-hand end of the Agora at Priene was the council-chamber (*bouleuterion*). This was the meeting-place of the city council (*boule*), which in most cities was an elected body numbering up to 500 men. The council prepared the business for the meetings of the assembly of citizens; and working in conjunction with the magistrates, it formed the state executive. It is extraordinary that in a city as small as Priene the council-chamber was built to house more than 500 people; but the prestige of the city must have required a building of this size. These council-chambers were arranged like indoor theatres. That at Priene had stone benches along three sides and a back door opening on to a higher street behind. As originally built in the third or second century B C it had a clear span of nearly 50 feet, which must have needed some form of truss-roofing; but when the roof was repaired the span was reduced by the introduction of internal supports.

Miletus had a more grandiose council-chamber, which was well situated at the focal point of the city and had a courtyard in front with a cloister for lobbying; this was donated at a relatively late stage in the city's building programme. The Hellenistic lay-out of Miletus was worthy of the birth-place of Hippodamus, the pioneer of city-planning. The model, based on the discoveries of the German excavators, gives a good impression of the city centre when the final touches had been given to it in Roman times – the baroque façades of the market gateway and public fountain belong to that era. But the general outlines of the lay-out go back to the original Hellenistic design. A great L-shaped zone was marked off for squares, markets and

Fig. 51

Plates 55, 56

Plate 75

public buildings; it ran from the wharves of the north harbour
southward for a quarter of a mile and then westward past the
second harbour, and so separated the residential quarters of the
town into three distinct complexes. Of the residential quarters
themselves less is known; in our present-day civilisation, whose
minimal requirement is 'sanitary dwellings with numbered
doors', the plumbing might appear primitive, but there are
lessons in planning to be learned from cities like Miletus.

Among the great public buildings of Miletus were a granary
over 500 feet long and a vast shopping stoa measuring no less
than 600 feet in length – the latter a donation of King Antiochus I of Syria. While the stoa may serve to remind us of the
generosity of the Kings towards the cities, the granary emphasises the need for adequate supplies of grain to feed the popula-

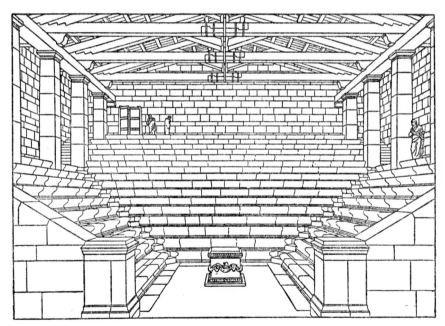

Fig. 51. Council Chamber of Priene. (From Krischen)

tion. Many of the cities did not grow enough wheat to feed themselves and depended on imports from South Russia or Egypt. It sometimes happened that in times of stress or drought demand exceeded supply and grain became unprocurable at a reasonable price. To meet such emergencies, to which decrees that come to light bear witness, some of the cities had corn-funds and appointed special commissioners to arrange in good time for the purchase of adequate stocks – at Samothrace it was ordained that the question of corn-stocks must be brought up on the agenda of the council every year on the 21st of the month Maimacterion. Often, too, when famine threatened a city and grain-prices soared, wealthy citizens would show their philanthropy by purchasing corn and distributing it free to their fellow-citizens or selling it at the normal price. Long afterwards the emperor Julian attempted to relieve a famine at Antioch in this way; but public morality had by then deteriorated, and the wealthy landowners kept their monopoly by buying up the whole of Julian's supply as soon as it came on to the market.

In the Hellenistic cities many individuals felt the need of smaller, less impersonal social groups and found satisfaction as members and officials of clubs which were generally dedicated to the cult of a god or hero; slaves often participated in these activities, while those of foreign origin joined together in the worship of the deities of their homelands, so that for instance we find in Rhodes an association of devotees of the Phrygian Moon God. The workers in different crafts and industries formed guilds in the cities; and foreign business-men who resided in the great commercial centres formed associations named after their own patron deities, like the Heracleistae of Tyre and the Syrian Adoniastae, or the Posidoniastae of Beirut, whose dedication of a statue-group in their club-house on Delos has survived as a monument of Hellenistic vulgarity.

In the designing of architectural masses and organisation of city life the professionals were the Attalid rulers of Pergamon.

Plate 52

THE
ATTALIDS

g. 52. Agora of Assos in bird's-eye view from the south-west. The foot of the citadel rock is at top left, the eatre bottom right. (From A. W. Lawrence, Greek Architecture*)*

'hey kept teams of skilled technicians and landscape gar-
:ners, and many cities benefited from their interest in public
orks. It was they, above all, who explored the possibilities
f superimposed building-masses on steep slopes. The little
)wn of Assos on the south coast of the Troad shows a typical
'ergamene arrangement. A huge flat-topped cone of basalt rises
om the coastal ridge, and this had formed the citadel of the
riginal Aeolic city. Much of the Hellenistic town lay where
ie Turkish village is now situated, on the relatively gentle
orth slope on the inland side of the ridge. But the main public
uildings were erected on the steep south slope above the little
arbour. A shallow natural terrace there was skilfully enlarged
) provide an Agora, flanked on either side by stoas built
gainst the slope. At the near end of this open space was a
:mple, at the far end were the council-chamber and public

Fig. 52

fountain. The stoa on the south presented a colonnaded façade to the Agora, while on the downhill side its substructures pro/ vided a row of shops opening on to a lower street. Being accus/ tomed to building on slopes, the Attalid architects seem by preference to have designed their stoas on terraces. And when Attalus II displayed his admiration for Athenian culture by donating a great stoa to close the east end of the Agora at Athens, his architects set the building on a high podium for the greater part of its length. This stoa has recently been rebuilt as a museum by the American excavators, and it well illus/ trates the splendour of Pergamene architecture and the design of a large stoa. There were rows of shops at the back of both storeys, and the broad colonnades provided space for the public to move up and down or take shelter from sun and storm. In stoas such as this the more publicly inclined philosophers addressed their audiences; and sometimes spaces were also par/ titioned off for meetings of public committees or courts.

Plate 54

Pergamon was a royal capital. It had its naval arsenal and port 15 miles away at Elaea, where the harbour mole, now standing derelict in a salt flat, must have been high enough to give access to the decks of big ships. The citadel of Pergamon itself was laid on the crest of a steep detached hill that dominates the flat valley of the Caicus. In the view of the German model we see the theatre on the steep slope to the left, with a buttressed promenade running at its foot. To the right of the theatre in this view stands the temple of Athena. The colonnaded build/ ing immediately behind was the library, the principal rival of the Alexandria Museum, with parchment rolls instead of papyrus; beyond this again is the conspicuous temple of Trajan, a late structure on a platform with vaulted substructures. To the right of the library is the palace; and at the back are the royal barracks, with the military arsenal in the extreme northern angle of the citadel. Water was brought from springs many miles away; from a reservoir tank on the opposite mountain/

Plate 58
Plate 57

side it was carried in metal pipes across a deep valley to ascend to the citadel and the upper parts of the town. Of the two large square complexes which descend the citadel slope to the south – in the foreground of the model – the lower one is an agora, while the upper one is the celebrated Great Altar. Public works such as these must have involved the destruction of existing properties; and we do find some evidence in the Greek cities of a system of expropriation and compensation. The god of insurance was Posidon, who in his capacity of Earth-shaker was the arbiter of hazards on land as well as at sea.

Some of the by-laws of Pergamon are known from a remark-able stone inscription discovered in 1901, on which were publicly engraved the duties of the Astynomoi, or junior magi-strates charged with police duties. It seems as if about two-fifths of the whole document is preserved; and though the existing inscription dates from Roman times, it must be a copy of an ordinance drawn up before 200 B C. This document shows how complex the regulations were; and since it has hitherto been misunderstood in some of its details, it may be worth while to give a synopsis of it here. The surviving text starts in the middle of an article concerning highways. Unauthorised obstructions shall be removed; if the offender does not comply, the Astynomoi must arrange for the removal within ten days and extract the cost from the culprit plus a 50 per cent fine. Main roads in the countryside must be at least 30 feet wide, minor roads not less than 12 feet wide (except for private foot-paths). Responsibility for keeping the roads clear and in good repair rests with the owners of properties within a zone of some furlongs back from the roadway. The rest of this column is missing; the next one is concerned with duties inside the city boundaries. If people throw refuse out of doors, the wardens of the city quarters must compel them to clear up the mess; if a warden is unsuccessful in doing so, he must call in the Astynomoi and they should arrange together for clearance to be made, charging the offender with the cost plus a fine of ten drachmae (about half a gold sovereign). If a warden neglects his duty the Astynomoi are to fine him twenty drachmae, such sums to be paid monthly into the special cleansing fund of the city treasury. If, however, the Astynomoi neglect these duties, the board of senior magistrates, in conjunction with the royal commissioner, are to fine them fifty drachmae for each offence. Penalties are then prescribed for digging up the roads for gravel and stones or scraping up mud to make plaster or bricks, and also for letting waste pipes discharge on the street surface – waste pipes should discharge underground into the public drain. If inhabitants of wards refuse to pay their share of the dung-collectors' charges or ward-penalties, the wardens must confiscate property of theirs and render an inventory of it within one day; if not reclaimed, the property will be officially auctioned after five days. The rest of this column of the text is missing.

What survives of the next column is entirely concerned with the problems of adjoining house properties. Where (perhaps in the interests of other parties) repairs are needed, the proprietors must take the necessary action; if one of two parties concerned demurs, the interested person is to take action in conjunction with the Astynomoi, and instead of paying the usual half the demurring party is charged three-fifths of the cost. In necessary repairs to common walls of adjoining properties the two neigh-bours pay equal shares if they use the wall equally. But if the wall has a building against it on one side and an open courtyard on the other side, they will pay in the proportion of two to one; and in the same proportion for two-storey buildings as against single-storey ones. People doing damage to common walls are responsible for repairs if the matter is referred to the Astynomoi and judgement is given against them. It is forbidden to build against common walls or undermine or damage them without the consent of all concerned. Similarly, trenches may not be dug along common walls or neighbours' walls, nor may butts be installed or trees planted against them; the Astynomoi are responsible for deciding whether an offence has been committed, and they must also deal with complaints about neighbours' walls which are in danger of collapse.

An unusual article in this column evidently relates to house properties on a steep slope. The accompanying sketch is intended to show one house higher up the slope than its neighbour. Along the common boundary line of the two properties

Fig. 53

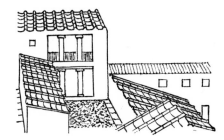

Fig. 53. Sketch to illustrate a By-law of Pergamon

the lower part of the wall of the right-hand house is backed against the filling on which the left-hand house stands, and we can understand that damp would seep through from the earth under the left-hand courtyard. The occupant of a lower house was therefore granted the right to dig a ventilation crack 18 inches wide along the edge of his neighbour's yard. The crack itself belonged to him; but the ground surface above it belonged to his neighbour. The crack must be covered with stone slabs, and its side must be revetted with a properly built wall unless there happened to be a filling of stones for the cover-slabs to rest on. The top of these cover-slabs must not rise above ground-level more than was necessary to allow rain-water to run off them. Ventilation cracks should have an entry from the owner's property. But occasionally this might not be possible; and if the city architect judged that it was impossible, the householder had the right of entry into his neighbour's yard for the purpose

of cleaning or repairing his crack. The final clause on this subject is not quite clear. It may simply be intended to safeguard
householders against tiresome neighbours who kept entering
their yard under cover of this regulation; but it may rather be
that such cracks would sometimes have their entry from a lane
at the front or back of the property and that vagrants might go
into the crack to commit a nuisance: whichever it was,
offenders brought before the Astynomoi and convicted were to
be fined five drachmae.

The last column of the royal law begins with responsibility
for keeping drains or conduits cleared, and then goes on to
fountains in the city and suburbs. The Astynomoi had the
responsibility for seeing that fountains were kept clean and that
the pipes and drains were not choked; if repairs became necessary, they must apply to the senior magistrates for a credit. It was
absolutely forbidden to water animals at public fountains and
to wash clothes or pans or anything else in them. Citizens
offending against this regulation were severely punished; the
animals or objects were confiscated and a fine of fifty drachmae
was imposed. But for house-slaves the penalty was corporal
punishment in addition to confiscation, and the punishment
was inhuman if the offence was committed without the
master's knowledge. Such emphasis was laid on keeping the
fountains clean that private persons making arrests were re-
warded with half of the proceeds. Cisterns in private houses
were to be registered and inspected annually to make sure that
they were watertight; the penalty for blocking one was one
hundred drachmae, while cisterns already blocked must be
cleared within eight months. The proceeds from these fines
were to go to a fund for constructing new cisterns (evidently at
the time of this law the rulers of Pergamon were not yet strong
enough to ignore the danger of a siege). The Astynomoi also
had strictly defined duties in connection with leaking cisterns
and compensation to neighbours suffering from the damp so

caused. Finally, the document breaks off in the middle of the regulations for public lavatories and their drainage.

This law shows professionals at work; and if it had survived complete we should have a very clear notion how a Hellenistic city was run. Regulations of this sort were not by any means confined to Pergamon. We may assume that the Eastern Greek cities as a whole took a pride in their cleanliness and public order, and that by defining neighbours' rights as closely as possible they sought to avoid unnecessary ill-feeling and litigation.

The Great Altar of Pergamon was erected as a monument of victory. The altar itself was not excessively large. But it was surrounded by a colonnaded court set on a podium and approached by a grand staircase 66 feet broad. Around the interior of the court ran a small frieze sculptured in a continuous narrative style that foreshadows the documentaries of the centenary columns of Trajan and Marcus Aurelius in Rome; it told the story of Telephus, whom the Kings of Pergamon had appropriated as the legendary founder of their city. The pride of Pergamene art, however, was the great frieze that ran round the exterior. This portrayed a battle of gods and giants which was deployed over a length of 370 feet on a scale considerably greater than lifesize. The earth-born giants force their massive bodies upwards into battle or fall back contorted in mortal agony. The sculptural plane heaves with the swirl of cloth and inflated muscles. Stones are hurled. Serpents hiss. Rent by hunting dogs and lions, the wounded giants groan; one is already on fire from the thunderbolt of Zeus. The noise must have been terrific. The subject is of course symbolic of the majesty of Pergamon mobilised in defence of civilisation.

Plates 59, 62

The first of the victories won by the Kings of Pergamon over the Galatians of Central Asia Minor had already been commemorated by a monument set up some time around 230 BC, from which two statue-groups seem to survive in marble copies.

Plate 61

These are the Dying Gaul of the Capitoline Museum and the Chieftain who evades capture by taking his wife's life and his own. The second of these works, with its novel design and powerful contrasts, must have been one of the masterpieces of third-century art. By their defiant aspect these statues of Gauls lent a savage grandeur to the vanquished barbarians and thereby enhanced the glory of the victor; and the artist who designed them had sufficient imagination to feel sympathy for the defeated. But when we turn back to the Great Altar, which was erected perhaps a couple of generations later, the difference is in fact profound. On the altar we see the work of a research team. The scholars of Pergamon have combed the Greek mythology so that 70 different deities – not to mention a like number of giants – could be depicted with their appropriate paraphernalia; and the artists in their turn have been at work exploring the range of physical and mental strains. The technique is magnificent. In this silent pandemonium the operatic poses and wardrobe effects of three centuries of art are combined in a single panorama. But the outcome is a triumph of virtuosity whose realism out-trumps reality.

FESTIVALS

People in the ancient world were not easily bored; and public spectacles and festal processions were always good entertainment. Some of the leading cities in Hellenistic times built huge

Plates 7, 63

temples, like that of Artemis at Sardis, or the temple of Apollo at Didyma whose oracular court and tall colonnades still stand in grandiose ruin; and the number of high-ranking athletic festivals was constantly increasing. The shrines of the healing gods were no less frequented. As people began to worry more about their health, the sanctuary of Asclepios on the island of Cos drew increasingly large crowds; and a complex of buildings was erected on a hill slope graded with three broad terraces which rose one behind the other. For an example of a small out-of-the-way cult we may glance at the hill-top sanctuary of the heroine Hemithea at a place called Kastabos in the south-west corner of Caria. This minor deity had become known for the miraculous cures that she performed; and towards the end of the fourth century a new temple was built for her in the Ionic order. Rhodes had annexed the territory here; the festival began to be widely known, and Diodorus tells us that huge concourses of pilgrims used to gather at the spot. A processional way 13 feet wide led up to the temple platform (on the left in the drawing, which has been based on British investigations there in 1959–60). Opposite the temple front were two build‑ ings, of which the larger may have served the needs of the clergy and the smaller may have been used for the display of venerable objects; the altar court was surrounded by a screen wall punctuated by tiny shrines, and after placing their offer‑ ings on the altar the invalids will have spent the night in the sacred enclosure hoping that the heroine would appear to make a cure. At the foot of the processional way there were buildings and esplanades, and below this was a theatre capable of offering entertainment for anything up to 10,000 people. The ordinary pilgrims no doubt camped out among the pine trees in the vicinity.

Plate 64

We learn from an inscription of the early second century B C that a crisis occurred at this out‑of‑the‑way sanctuary, because the crowds became too great to be accommodated in so confined a spot; but unfortunately the text is hopelessly worn, so it is not now clear how the situation was remedied. We can, however, recapture some of the excitement that was felt in such tightly pressed throngs by ourselves attending similar gatherings at festivals in modern Greece, or from snatches of conversation like these in an Alexandrian idyll of Theocritus:

'For goodness sake, don't knock me down. What a mercy we left the baby at home!'
'Will we manage to get inside?'
'Everything is done by trying, dearie. It was by trying that the Achaeans got inside Troy.'

'What sermons that old girl preaches!'

'Oh, there's nothing women don't know; they can even tell you what Zeus did when he first made love to Hera.'

'Just look, Praxinoa. What a crowd round the doors!'

'Good heavens! Gorgo, give me your hand. And Eunoa hang on to Eutychis. Hold tight so you don't get lost.'

'Oh dear, that's my summer dress split right in two. My dear man, as you wish to be saved, take care with my shawl.'

'I can't help it, but I'll do all I can.'

'What a crowd! They are all shoving like pigs.'

'Don't worry, madam. We are safely through now.'

'Blessings on you now and hereafter, sir, for looking after us. What an obliging gentleman that was! Now we are all safely inside, as the man said when he shut his bride out.'

'Praxinoa, just look at those embroideries. . . . Hush, the girl is starting to sing. . . .'

'Very pretty! But it's time to be going home. My husband hasn't had his breakfast yet.'

In this chapter we have seen the conditions under which the Hellenistic way of life was lived. It was pre-eminently a city life, and it transcended national boundaries and racial sentiment. Perhaps the most remarkable thing about this cosmopolitan age is the contribution that the newly hellenised cities made to Greek culture. The noble Stoic doctrine of the brotherhood of mankind was first preached by a Cypro-Phoenician, Zeno, in Athens; and the most distinguished of his successors came from cities like Tarsus or Soli in Cilicia and Seleucia on the Tigris. The famous physicist Seleucus belonged to another Seleucia on the Persian Gulf; Crates, the scholarly librarian of Pergamon, came from Cilician Mallus, and the great geometrician Apollonius was a Pamphylian of Perge. Famous Hellenistic thinkers and historians came from Phoenician Byblos, Apamea on the Orontes, Amasia in Pontus, Ascalon, Antioch-Nisibis in Kurdistan, Artemita in Babylonia, and

Damascus; the Scriptures were translated and studied at Alexandria, where Jews had been invited to settle as citizens and
given their own ghetto. Among the leading literary figures of
the age were Aratus of Soli, Meleager of Gadara near the
borders of Galilee, Antipater of Sidon, and at a later date
Lucian from the barely hellenised town of Samosata on the
upper Euphrates. It is true that poetry and rhetoric were
gradually sinking into gilded artificiality, and genius was
giving way to systematisation of scholarship; but these qualities
were by no means despicable, and no achievement of the
Hellenistic Age is more impressive than the brotherhood of
classical Greek culture, learning and belles-lettres that sprang
up among people whose ancestors had not known Greek. In
the country districts of the newly hellenised lands Hellenism
did not penetrate quickly. In Asia Minor it eventually triumphed, and Cappadocia and Pontus were among its chief
strongholds. But the religious conservatism of Judaea reacted
against hellenisation. Aramaic survived there, and in Syria also
it continued to be spoken; and thus Syriac, like Coptic, came
to be a language of the Christian liturgy.

CHAPTER XV

Roman Recessional

WE MAY IF WE WISH believe – as Livy would have us believe – that the Romans conquered their entire empire in self-defence, or at least out of a sense of justice and fair play. There was always another oppressed people to be succoured or a more distant enemy who needed humbling; and so the Roman Empire grew by a chain of circumstances that in retrospect at least seems inevitable. Philip V of Macedon and Antiochus the Great were crushed. Eumenes II of Pergamon and the Rhodian republic had been Rome's allies; but once the more formidable enemies had been overcome, they in their turn were too con⁄ spicuous and had to be humiliated. And, on the other side of the Aegean, Greece was finally reduced to impotence by Roman arms. The effect of this heavy⁄handed intervention on the political initiative of the Hellenistic states was stultifying. Attalus III recognised the futility of trying to postpone the inevitable outcome. He made Rome his heir; and after his death in 133 BC the kingdom of Pergamon became a Roman province. Before long, Italian business corporations were com⁄ peting with provincial governors for the profits of Roman rule; Italian capital was invested in the neighbouring kingdom of Bithynia, and the independent spirit of the ruler of Pontus soon appeared as a cause of offence.

Plate 65g
Mithridates VI of Pontus was descended from a noble Persian family; and a natural impetuosity, combined with the traditional Iranian virtues and a Greek cultural background, mark him out as the last picturesque monarch of free Anatolia. Neither he nor the Roman Senate wished to become involved in a major war. But there was not room in Asia Minor for Mithridates' ambition as well as Italian business interests. When war at last came in the year 88 BC, the King swept through the

province of Asia; he was hailed as a liberator by the Greeks, and at his command tens of thousands of Italians were massacred. For a moment there was jubilation. But Mithridates could not hold what he had won; and it was only because of the many distractions that beset Rome as a world power that he was able for a quarter of a century to maintain a state of uneasy peace or open defiance. Eventually, in 66 B C, he was driven out of Asia Minor to his last refuge in the Crimea; and Pompey the Great thereupon laid the foundations of a lasting settlement in which all Asia up to the Euphrates was brought under direct or indirect Roman rule.

'It was artfully contrived by Augustus that in the enjoyment of plenty the Romans should lose the memory of freedom.' When he delivered himself of this judgement, Gibbon may have done an injustice to the first emperor's aims, but as the historian of Empire he did not mistake the consequence of his actions. Internal war was at an end; and not only Rome but the whole Empire came to look to the Palatine as the source of all government. Thanks to what the Greeks had done, the Empire as a political unity was not so much a collection of provinces as a vast network of cities whose status was that of municipalities. The cities were the centres of education and culture; and to a large extent they relieved the imperial government of the burdens of administration and assumed responsibility for security, communications and taxcollection. As a way of life the Greek city triumphed; indeed, it was so selfassured in its cultural heritage that practically speaking no Greek ever heard the names of Horace or Virgil. But politically it had to stomach the loss of the independence it had so long fought for; and there was perhaps a certain wryness in the remark of the unctuous Aelius Aristides that 'of course, it is more blessed to pay taxes to Rome than to receive tribute from others.'

Publius Aelius Aristides was the spokesman for the Greeks of his age. Born in the Mysian backwoods where city life was

EMPIRE ON
HOLIDAY

introduced about the time of his birth by the emperor Hadrian, he settled at Smyrna and with the help of a strong constitution devoted himself to the care of his health. He nevertheless found leisure for rhetorical exercises, and the address that he delivered to the Romans about A D 143 strikes the keynote of the 'Golden Age': 'As though on holiday,' he tells the Romans, 'the world has shed its burden of arms and devotes itself freely to beautifica, tion and festivity of every kind. The cities have relinquished their old feuds; and a single rivalry possesses every one of them – to be the best and most beautiful of all. Everywhere are gym, nasia, fountains, arches, temples, town halls and schools. The ailing world has been, so to speak, scientifically restored to complete health. Donations flow perpetually from you to the cities; and no one can tell who gets the largest share because your bounty is so impartial. The cities positively gleam with radiance and charm, and the whole earth is a pleasure garden. The smoke of burning homes and warning beacons is gone with the wind from the face of land and sea; instead we are confronted with spectacles of manifold charm and an infinitude of public games. Thus, unquenchable like a sacred flame, the fair never stops but passes on from place to place; and it is always continuing somewhere, for the whole world has quali, fied for these blessings.'

They had never had it so good. 'There is no need of garrisons in the cities, because in each one the greatest and most powerful of the citizens act as Rome's guardians. . . . The masses are protected from the powerful ones by the authority of Rome, so that rich and poor are equally contented and equally benefited.' This amicable concord was part of the system that Roman rule had built up in the provinces. The wealth became concen, trated in the hands of a few leading families. These were Rome's friends; they acquired Roman citizenship and, like Aristides himself, two Latin names; and local government was firmly placed in their hands. They did not always exert their powers for the benefit of the whole community. Those who wielded power in the cities must often have been torn between two conflicting ambitions – to use the public funds to make their cities more impressive, or to enlarge their own private fortunes. We occasionally read of popular indignation against magnates who contributed too little for improvements or enter-tainments in their cities; and though public works and spec-tacles were not the only legitimate objects of expenditure, the surviving remains and inscriptions of the cities are often a good index of the social conscience that prevailed.

In Bithynia and Pontus very little trace survives of the famous cities – even of Nicomedia and Nicaea which kept up a bitter rivalry for precedence in the province. As against this, we have an authoritative record of conditions there in the correspondence of Pliny the Younger, who was sent out by Trajan in the year 111 as a special commissioner to correct abuses. Before Pliny's arrival, public works had been sanctioned on a con-siderable scale in several cities and the money had been paid out from the city treasuries; but there was surprisingly little to show for it all. Nicomedia had spent the equivalent of some tens of thousands of gold pounds on two successive schemes for an aqueduct, and both had been abandoned. At Nicaea the sub-structures laid for a theatre were condemned as unsound after £100,000 had been spent on them. Leading citizens were owing large sums to the treasuries, and they had been refusing to pay the fees due from them. There was a reluctance in some places to submit accounts for scrutiny; and from Pliny's ingenuous statement the experienced emperor had no difficulty in surmising that money paid out for public works had been going into private pockets. We have also an interesting side-light on imperial policy in the correspondence. A fire had raged unchecked in Nicomedia and destroyed many buildings, and Pliny recommended that a fire brigade should be formed. But Trajan forbade this on grounds of public policy; for he feared that – as happened in American towns of the nineteenth cen, tury – the fire brigades would develop into well, organised political clubs. On the other hand the practical emperor, who was so much concerned with waterways, was greatly interested by the Nicomedians' project of cutting a canal to connect their lake by locks with the sea.

In Bithynia we see the evil effects of the Roman system. By way of contrast, the public buildings and civic munificence of the cities of the south coast of Asia Minor cannot fail to excite our admiration. The cities there had handsome shopping avenues flanked by broad side, walks under the shelter of colon, nades. They had grand theatres and vaulted stadiums, orna, mental gateways, and monumental buildings inside the wall circuit. Here, as in the leading cities of Ionia, Aelius Aristides' sermon is not belied; and granting that the southern cities have been fortunate in the chances of survival, it seems nevertheless true that the very ruins of a place like Pamphylian Perge amount to more than the magnates of Nicaea ever erected. At the neigh, bouring site of Aspendus, which was never a city of much consequence, a theatre over 300 feet across was built out at the foot of the citadel hill in the second century after Christ; made of local stone by a local architect, it has successfully withstood time and the elements; and only the loss of the marble facing of the stage background mars the clean lines of the original con, struction. Half a mile away, the ruined aqueduct, with its single tier of arches, still courses for many hundreds of yards across the plain. As it approached the citadel, the water was piped up to a tank raised on arches 100 feet above ground level, and from there it was carried by normal flow into the town.

Cyprus and Phoenicia flourished under Roman rule. Egypt, won from the Ptolemies, was the emperor's special domain. Never at rest, Judaea blew up in the time of Hadrian. South of the Dead Sea, in the region of the rift valley that extends to the Gulf of Akaba, the wilderness had once been awakened to

Plates 66, 67

Plate 68

Plate 69

agricultural and industrial life by Solomon. After the time of Alexander the Great it was brought to life again by the Nabataean Arabs, who commanded the caravan routes centring on Petra and by their works of water conservancy made the desert habitable. Allied to Rome, they were only brought inside the Empire in AD 106.

Coele Syria between the Orontes and Jordan valleys belonged to the Ituraean Arabs and had relatively little urban development. But in Roman times a colony was formed at Ba'albek, whose Greek name was Heliopolis (City of the Sun); and here on the watershed between Lebanon and Antilebanon a huge sanctuary was built. In terms of sheer acreage, weight of stone, dimensions of individual blocks, and the amount of carving, this precinct can scarcely have had a rival in the Graeco-Roman world.

The sacred enclosure of Ba'albek measured about 300 yards in length, the whole forming a great platform. At the east end stood a propylaea between two towers, approached by a stairway 150 feet broad. Inside this was a hexagonal forecourt giving access to the main temple court. The latter was surrounded by a colonnade, behind which the wall was diversified by alternating semicircular and oblong bays fronted by columns. The west side of this court was closed by the great temple of Ba'al, which was 100 yards long and stood on a podium 45 feet high. A row of half a dozen columns 65 feet high still stands in position, and the entablature over them is elaborately carved; but so little else remains of this gigantic structure that the visitor is left wondering whether it was ever more than a fragment. Alongside this podium a smaller temple was erected at a lower level; and this second building, itself no smaller than the Parthenon, is still standing almost intact. Its spacious interior is articulated by engaged Corinthian columns; they carry a complete entablature on which the ceiling rested, and between them were arched and gabled niches which will have

Plates 70, 71

Plate 72

Plate 73

Plate 74

Plate 75

DECLINE OF
CITY LIFE

enshrined statues of deities. Finally, outside the precinct stood a little temple which consisted of a circular cella entered through a normal porch. This little building shows some architectural subtlety; the outer columns of the rotunda carried a lunate entablature which helped to take the thrust of the dome; and the capitals, cut with five sides to conform to the unusual design, reproduce on a smaller scale the arcs of the entablature above.

The architects employed at Ba'albek were no doubt skilled in their profession; indeed, the neighbouring city of Damascus produced the most famous architect of Trajan's reign. The workmanship at Ba'albek was equal to the best of its time; and the architectural façades will have been enlivened by innumerable statues in the niches. Yet the sheer opulence and endless repetition of the same motifs of imperial baroque induce in the spectator a feeling of satiety. The Roman world was incomparable in its engineering; but in its artistic sensibility, as in its taste for food and literature, it had a unique immunity from any feeling of indigestion. Magnificence was an end in itself, irrespective of what might lie behind; and it is characteristic of Roman imperial architecture that the same grandiose façade, with its ornate composite or Corinthian order and twostoreyed bays and niches, could with scarcely any modification serve for a gateway, a theatre scene, a city fountain, a public library, or simply as a screen to exclude the outer world.

In North Syria the great city was Antioch. Life there must have been very attractive in the second century after Christ; and, with the river traffic, the festivals, and the pleasure grove and mosaicfloored villas of the rich suburb of Daphne, it could still be gracious in the fourth. We are fortunate in knowing about conditions there from the writings of Libanius, who spent the second half of his life as professor in his native city between the years 354 and 393. The tragedy of Antioch in his time was the attrition of the 'curial' families in the city.

Membership of the city council (or *curia*), in Antioch and other places, had been made hereditary; and what had once been esteemed a privilege had long since become a burden. The wealthiest members of this class found an escape by buying their way into the governing aristocracy of the Empire, and conse-quently their estates ceased to contribute, so to speak, to the city rates. An increasingly heavy burden was thus laid on the curial families of more moderate means; and the governing class in the cities began to degenerate into a caste of petty officials. They could no longer keep up the former standard of civic munifi-cence and they lacked the authority to control the popular riots. Many of the cities must have collapsed under the strain – places, for instance, like Cnidus on its barren headland, where the maintenance of public services depended on a brisk com-merce; and in other places the citizens lived among the ruins of buildings that they could no longer keep in repair. But life had its dignity still in the larger cities; and the Church com-forted the poor with the assurance that they were equal in the sight of God, and to some extent also helped to carry the burden of philanthropy.

Libanius gives a not altogether unsympathetic picture of the curial families who still retained something of the old values in the decay of their class. Thanks to them, of course, food supply and public shows were maintained; but it was thanks to them also that education and civic amenities survived. In the Western provinces of the Empire city life gave way to feudal organisation. But in the East, where their traditions were stronger, the cities held their place in the bureaucratic system of the Byzantine Empire.

In Egypt and Syria the Greek cities were extinguished with the Arab conquest. In Asia Minor they lasted longer; the diminutive realm of Trebizond held out until 1461; and Christian communities, like those of Smyrna, the Pontus and Cappadocian Caesarea, subsisted until the disaster of only 40 years ago. But, in general, the Greek city as the relic of a self-governing institution came to an end in Asia Minor in the generations around A D 1300 when the Turkish Ghazis broke through the Seljuk empire to establish new principalities along the coasts; and it had been in decay for a long time before that. At Ephesus, for instance, the harbour had silted up and the dwindling city had begun to take shelter at the shrine of St John the Theologian, from which it received its medieval name. It fell in A D 1304. To the Franks of the fourteenth century it was the seat of a Turkish emir from whom they desired trading concessions. The ancient glory of Ephesus was forgotten; and even the new name Ay Theológos ceased to be understood, for in our medieval sources it figures as Altoluogo, Hautelogie, Latolongo, 'altus locus' and 'alter locus', and finally descends to 'aultres lieux de Turquie'.

The fortunes of the Greek cities of Asia in the Middle Ages do not count as having a place in world history – not even the fate of the former Attalid foundation of Philadelphia, whose Christian inhabitants remembered the words that 'He that Shutteth and no man can Open' had addressed to their church, and held their Door in the face of the Turks for almost a hundred years after the neighbouring cities of Asia had fallen. But that old Ionic invention, the Greek City, had long since fulfilled its historical rôle. Attenuated though it was, the Eastern Empire had survived; and the Western World was ready to receive the heritage of Greek culture and humanism.

Bibliography

Books cited without an asterisk should be intelligible to general readers.
*Works demanding some background knowledge.
**More specialized works.

Primary reports of excavations and field researches are too numerous to be listed here; the most accessible recent bibliography is that in A. W. Lawrence's *Greek Architecture,* pp. 307–16.

The list is primarily intended for readers whose native tongue is English. On the general topics there are standard works in French and German which are not cited here.

Asia Minor before the Greeks

SETON LLOYD, *Early Anatolia,* Penguin Books 1956.

O. R. GURNEY, *The Hittites,* Penguin Books 1952.

General History of Greece until Alexander the Great

J. B. BURY, *History of Greece to the Death of Alexander the Great,* revised by Russell Meiggs, Macmillan 1955.

R. M. COOK, *The Greeks till Alexander,* Thames & Hudson 1962.

N. G. L. HAMMOND, *History of Greece to 322 BC,* Oxford, Clarendon 1959.

The Cambridge Ancient History, Cambridge Univ. 1923– .

Early History

GREECE AS A WHOLE

A. R. BURN, *The Lyric Age of Greece,* E. Arnold 1960.
CHESTER G. STARR, *The Origins of Greek Civilization,* New York, Borzoi Books 1961.

Bibliography

IONIA **F. BILABEL, *Die Ionische Kolonisation*, Leipzig, Dieterich 1920.

**F. CASSOLA, *La Ionia nel Mondo Miceneo*, Naples, Edizioni Scientifiche Italiane 1957.

*C. ROEBUCK, *Ionian Trade and Colonization*, New York, Archaeological Institute of America 1959.

**M. B. SAKELLARIOU, *La Migration Grecque en Ionie*, Athens, Institut Français 1958.

GREEKS IN THE EAST AND PEOPLES OF NEARER ASIA Ctesias, edited with French translation, R. HENRY, *Ctésias, La Perse, l'Inde*, Brussels, J. Lebègue 1947.

Herodotus (available in translations).

*T. J. DUNBABIN, *The Greeks and their Eastern Neighbours*, London, Society for Promotion of Hellenic Studies 1957.

R. GHIRSHMAN, *Iran*, Penguin Books 1954.

A. T. OLMSTEAD, *History of the Persian Empire*, Chicago Univ. 1948, 1959.

Persepolis Sculptures (full record):
E. F. SCHMIDT, *Persepolis* vol. I, Chicago Univ. 1951.

The Ten Thousand:
Xenophon, *Anabasis* = *Expeditio Cyri* (available in translations).

History and Geography of the Hellenistic East

GENERAL Diodorus Siculus, books 17–20 (translation in Loeb Classical Library).

*Strabo, *Geographica*, books 11–17 (translation in Loeb Classical Library).

The Cambridge Ancient History vols. VI–VIII, (1927–30).

A. H. M. JONES, *The Greek City from Alexander to Justinian*, Oxford, Clarendon 1940.

**W. M. RAMSAY, *Historical Geography of Asia Minor*, Murray 1890.

*M. Rostovtzeff, *The Social and Economic History of the Hellenistic World*, 3 vols., Oxford, Clarendon 1953.

W. W. Tarn and G. T. Griffith, *Hellenistic Civilization*, E. Arnold 1952.

Arrian, *Anabasis of Alexander* (available in translations).

**E. Bikerman, *Les Institutions des Séleucides*, Paris, P. Geuthner 1938.

*C. J. Cadoux, *Ancient Smyrna*, Oxford, Blackwell 1938.

*Glanville Downey, *History of Antioch in Syria*, Princeton Univ. 1961.

**P. M. Fraser and G. E. Bean, *The Rhodian Peraea and Islands*, Oxford Univ. 1954.

**H. van Gelder, *Geschichte der alten Rhodier*, Hague, M. Nijhoff 1900.

*Esther V. Hansen, *The Attalids of Pergamon*, Cornell Univ. 1947.

A. K. Narain, *The Indo-Greeks*, Oxford, Clarendon 1957.

W. W. Tarn, *The Greeks in Bactria and India*, Cambridge Univ. 1938.

W. W. Tarn, *Alexander the Great* vol. I, notes and appendices in vol. II, Cambridge Univ. 1948.

Archaeology, Architecture and Art

Ekrem Akurgal, *Die Kunst Anatoliens von Homer bis Alexander*, Berlin, de Gruyter 1961.

Ekrem Akurgal, *Phrygische Kunst*, Ankara 1955.

J. M. Cook, *Greek Archaeology in Western Asia Minor* in 'Archaeological Reports', London, Society for Promotion of Hellenic Studies 1960.

R. M. Cook, *Greek Painted Pottery*, Methuen 1960.

H. Frankfort, *Art and Architecture of the Ancient Orient*, Penguin Books 1954.

A. W. Lawrence, *Later Greek Sculpture*, J. Cape 1927.

Bibliography

A. W. LAWRENCE, *Greek Architecture,* Penguin Books 1957.

ROLAND MARTIN, *L'Urbanisme dans la Grèce Antique,* Paris, A. & J. Picard 1956.

F. MILTNER, *Ephesos,* Vienna, F. Deuticke 1958.

M. ROSTOVTZEFF, *Dura-Europos and its Art,* Oxford, Clarendon 1938.

HANS SCHRADER, *Archaische griechische Plastik,* Breslau, F. Hirt 1933.

M. SCHEDE, *Die Ruinen von Priene, Kurze Beschreibung,* Berlin, de Gruyter 1934.

R. E. WYCHERLEY, *How the Greeks built Cities,* Macmillan 1949.

Science, Thought and Exploration

MAX CARY and E. H. WARMINGTON, *The Ancient Explorers,* Methuen 1929.

BENJAMIN FARRINGTON, *Greek Science,* 2 vols., Penguin Books Part I 1944, 1949, Part II 1949; single-volume edition 1953, 1961.

*G. S. KIRK and J. E. RAVEN, *The Presocratic Philosophers,* Cambridge Univ. 1957.

WILFRED H. SCHOFF, *The Periplus of the Erythraean Sea, Travel and Trade in the Indian Ocean by a Merchant of the First Century,* Longmans Green 1912.

1

2

3

4

5

6

7

9

10

13   11

12

14

15

6

17

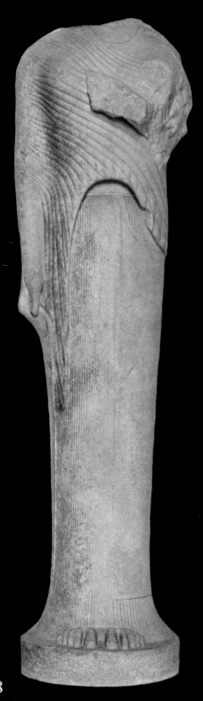

18

19

21

22

23

24

26

27

28

9

1

30

34

39

40

43

14

45

46

47

51

MVNIFIC

53

54

55

56

57

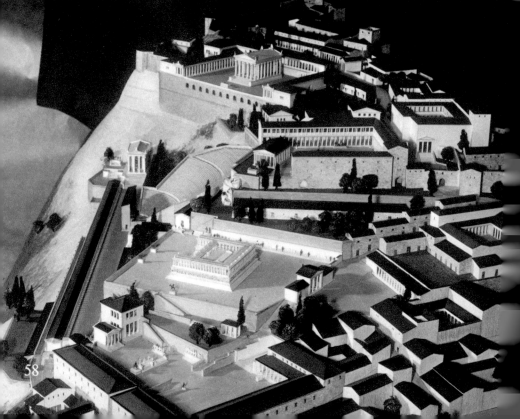

58

HP. Feb. '61

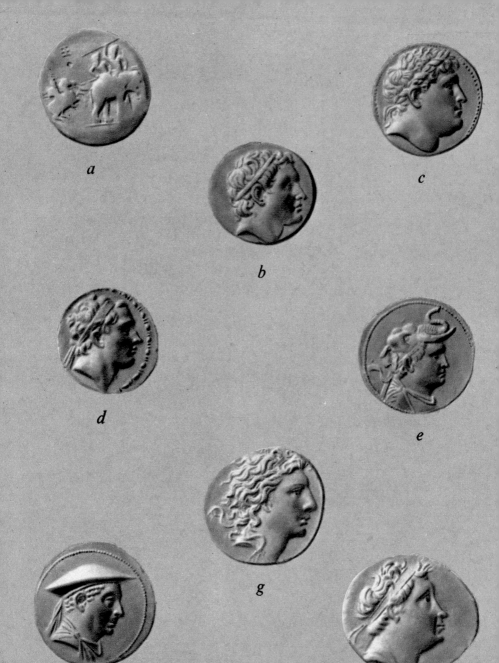

a

b

c

d

e

f

g

h

66

67

68

69

70

71

73

74

75

76

NOTES ON THE PLATES

Notes on the Plates

1 Rock-relief of a goddess, at Akpinar on the north foot of Mt Sipylus in-land from Smyrna. Height about 15 ft, probably Late Bronze Age.

2 Rock-relief of a warrior (probably the god Teshub), wearing boots and horned cap and armed with bow, sword and spear (or staff), in the Kara-bel Pass inland from Smyrna; the hieroglyphs in front of the figure speak of a great king, but the name cannot be read. Probably Hittite. Height about 9 ft.

3-4 Ruins of houses at Alâzeytin on the Halicarnassus peninsula. This Carian hill-top town was abandoned about 360 BC. Photographs by G. E. Bean.

5 Site of the ancient Lebedos, a small city of the Ionic coast.

6 Ionic town of Myonnesus, view from the peninsula-site down onto the isthmus.

7 Citadel of Sardis, seen from the Great Temple. Photograph by Max Hirmer.

8 Inlaid screen, probably of boxwood; one of a pair found leaning against the inner wall of the cabin in the great tumulus of Gordion. Height just over 3 ft, late eighth century BC. The bronze bossed phiale is of a form imitated in Greece in the seventh and sixth centuries. Photograph pro-vided by R. S. Young.

9 Entrance way and south side of the sanctuary precinct at Old Smyrna, late seventh century BC. The old temple lay behind the tree stump on the right.

Notes on the Plates

10   Gold ornament in the form of a stag, from Kul Oba in the Crimea, in the Hermitage Museum. Greek workmanship of about 500 BC. Length about 12 in. Photograph by courtesy of the Society for Cultural Relations with the U.S.S.R.

11   Mouldings crowning a marble round altar in Samos, diameter 2 ft 8 in.; middle or third quarter of the sixth century BC. Photograph by R. V. Nicholls.

12   Ionic capital of the Artemisium of Ephesus, British Museum restoration; mid sixth century BC. The low moulded shelf at the top (abacus) is unusual in early Ionic. Museum photograph.

13   Detail of tufa capital from temple at Old Smyrna, late seventh century BC.

14-15   Rhodian terracotta flask for scented oil, in the form of a lady of fashion bearing an offering of a pigeon; from Camirus (Rhodes), now in the British Museum. Height 10 in., second half of the sixth century BC. Museum photographs.

16   Painted vase (oenochoe) found in a seventh-century house at Old Smyrna. Lion, boar and wild goat above; goat hunt below. Probably made in Chios about 625 BC.

17   Ivory relief-plaque found at the Samian Heraeum; Perseus killing the Gorgon, with Athena on the left lending a hand. Photograph by German Archaeological Institute, Athens.

18-19   Marble statue dedicated to Hera by Cheramyes, found at the Samian Heraeum, now in the Louvre. Height 6 ft 4 in., second quarter of the sixth century BC. Photographs by Max Hirmer.

20-21   Marble statue of a gentleman in Samos. Height 6 ft, mid sixth century BC. Photograph by German Archaeological Institute, Athens.

22 Upper part of marble statue of a lady, dedicated on the Acropolis at Athens, but believed to be of Chian workmanship; Acropolis Museum No. 675. Half lifesize, about 520 BC. Photograph by Max Hirmer.

23 Marble head of a lady. Berlin Museums; from Asia Minor. Date a little after 550 BC. Museum photograph.

24 Marble figure of a lion, Berlin Museums; from Asia Minor. It may have been set as a guardian over a tomb. Length 5 ft 6 in., third quarter of the sixth century BC. Museum photograph.

25 Marble figure from Didyma, believed to be from the base-drum of a column of the old temple; Berlin Museums, about 530 BC. Museum photograph.

26 'Fikellura' amphora from Rhodes, British Museum. Height 13 in., mid sixth century BC. Museum photograph.

27 Black-figured vase in Munich, one of four closely related amphorae collectively known as the 'Northampton Group'. The horses get at the wine bowl. Probably made in Italy about 535 BC. Pieces found in Smyrna and South Russia seem to be earlier works of the same artist; and if that is so, he may have been a Phocaean who emigrated to Italy at the time of the Persian conquest. Museum photograph.

28 Small fragment from a 'Clazomenian' vase, in Berlin Museums. A herald (?) with staff and censer in front of an enthroned couple (Priam and Hecuba?), with a chariot approaching. About 540 BC. Photograph by R. M. Cook.

29–30 'Caeretan' hydria from Caere in South Etruria, in the Louvre. Height 17 in., about 525 BC. The figured scene shows Apollo arguing with the parents of Hermes in their cave on Mt Cyllene. Apollo has been searching for his cattle, which are seen looking out of the bushes on the left; the infant Hermes, who has stolen them, now lies in bed on a trolley while his parents protest his innocence. Giraudon photographs.

31 Fragmentary 'Caeretan' hydria in the British Museum. An Arimaspian drives away with a haversack of gold, pursued by a griffin who is quivering with rage. Museum photograph.

32 'Clazomenian' sarcophagus in the Berlin Museums, late sixth century BC. Red figure at head end (winged goddess and cavalrymen, centaurs with poles), Black figure at foot (goats, lion and panther). From *Antike Denkmäler*.

33 Detail of sarcophagus found in the vicinity of Old Smyrna, in Smyrna Museum (by courtesy of the Director). Sphinx wearing jewellery. Late sixth century BC.

34 Four small bronzes. Mouse, flying fish, pony and man ploughing with two oxen (the reversed ox may signalize the turn at the end of the furrow). Finlay Collection, British School at Athens, said to have been found at Çeşme, west of Smyrna. The British Museum and Fitzwilliam Museum, Cambridge, possess other bronzes of the same group. Sixth century BC.

35 View inside Polycrates' tunnel at Samos, a little distance from the south end. Photograph by E. J. André Kenny.

36 Glazed tile relief from Darius' palace at Susa, now in the Louvre. Persian guardsmen of the Household Brigade ('Immortals'). Museum photograph.

37 Persepolis, East Stairway of the Apadana. The reliefs show guardsmen and courtiers in procession. Photograph by the Oriental Institute, Chicago.

38 Persepolis terrace, the Syrian delegation to the New Year festival. Photograph by the Oriental Institute, Chicago.

39–40 Fortifications of Assos in the Troad, showing the tower-flanked main gateway (40) and a smaller gate (39). Squared masonry; probably of the second quarter of the fourth century BC, but these fortifications have not received serious study. A banker named Eubulus made himself master of

Assos and the neighbouring Atarneus; besieged in one of his strongholds by a satrap in the revolt of the 360's, he is said to have made his enemy calculate the cost of starving him out and then offered to sell the place at a discount. Eubulus was succeeded by his former slave Hermias, who married his niece to Aristotle and ran the principality as a Platonic limited company until he was betrayed to Artaxerxes Ochus about 345 BC. Photographs by G. E. Bean.

41 Site of Cnidus, view west from the citadel slope to the 'island'. On the left, the commercial harbour; across the isthmus, on the right, the naval harbour. The lines of ancient building terraces can be seen on the 'island'. Photograph by R. V. Nicholls.

42 Cnidus. View from the 'island' north-east across the naval harbour, whose entrance was defended by bastions. The city wall followed the jagged crest in the upper right part of the picture. The building terraces inside the city circuit were explored by C. T. Newton in 1857–59. Photograph by R. V. Nicholls.

43 Demeter of Cnidus, in the British Museum. The whole seated figure is 5 ft high; about 330 BC.

44 Marble statue from the Mausoleum of Halicarnassus, now in the British Museum. Height of figure 10 ft, about 350 BC. The man is of an un-Greek appearance and probably Mausolus himself. Photograph by Max Hirmer.

45–46 Alexander the Great and Darius. Details from a four-colour mosaic from Pompeii, now in Naples Museum. Probably based on the painting of 'Alexander's Battle with Darius' by Philoxenus of Eretria. As his chariot swings round in flight, Darius reaches out his hand towards a Persian noble (not shown here) who has interposed his body between his King and Alexander's spear. It is not known whether the battle shown here is Issus or Gaugamela. Alinari photographs.

47 Ruined viaduct on the ancient highroad 2½ hours east of Cnidus. Its total length was about 220 ft and its width 25 ft. The narrow triangular

opening for the torrent was 10 ft wide at the bottom; its left edge can be seen in the picture. Probably built soon after 334 BC. Photograph by G. E. Bean.

48 Bronze statue of an Iranian chief or Parthian satrap, wearing diadem and torque; found at Shami in Susiana, now in Teheran Museum. Height 6 ft 6 in., probably late Hellenistic. Photograph by courtesy of A. N. Sherwin White.

49–50 The unique burial ground of Antiochus I of Commagene, on top of the 7,000-ft-high Nemrud Daǧı west of the Euphrates; first half of the first century BC. Plate 50 shows the row of colossal images of native deities on the East Terrace, with the great tumulus behind; the two people on the lap of the 'Goddess Commagene' give the scale. Plate 49 shows the head of Heracles Artagnes from the West Terrace; it is over 6 ft high. Photographs provided by F. K. Dörner.

51 Small-scale marble replica of the 'Tyche' (Fortune) of Antioch, in the Vatican. The goddess wears a mural crown and rests her foot on the river Orontes. The original statue, of the time of the foundation of Antioch, was the work of Eutychidas. Alinari photograph.

52 Statue group from the club house of the Beirutî merchants at Delos. Aphrodite, posed for her bath, playfully threatens to use her slipper upon an amorous old Pan, while Eros joins in the fun. Height 4 ft 6 in., about 100 BC. Photograph by courtesy of the Greek Directorate of Antiquities.

53 Model of the lower town at Priene, Berlin Museums; view from the south-west. Museum photograph.

54 Model of north end of the Stoa of Attalus at Athens, built by Attalus II of Pergamon (159–138 BC). 382 ft long, and 64 ft from front to back, with a promenade 20 ft broad at the front. Doric and Ionic orders on the façade, Ionic and Pergamene capitals inside. Photograph provided by American School of Classical Studies, Athens.

55-56   Miletus, model of the 'Lion Harbour' and city centre, Berlin Museums. The upper view shows the harbour head from the north. On the water-front, to left, a large Roman bath building and (beyond the trees) the colonnaded courtyard of Delphinian Apollo, where public inscriptions were kept. On the right of the waterfront, a sea victory monument, with the long façade of a Hellenistic stoa behind. Beyond this (in line behind the big ship) is the North Agora, flanked by colonnades and shops, and on the left of this is a broad paved boulevard with sidewalks. The public buildings at the back appear in the lower photograph (56), which shows the little central piazza from the east, with the boulevard leading off from it on the four o'clock ray. On the near side of the boulevard, at right bot-tom, is the two-storeyed courtyard of a Roman bath building, and to the left of this a Hellenistic gymnasium with its main hall, court and porch; opposite the porch is the end of the Nymphaeum (a monumental fountain fed by an aqueduct on arches). Beyond this is the ornamental gateway (Plate 75) leading into the great South Agora (not completed in the model); the Stoa of Antiochus I led off from the left corner of the gateway. Across the little piazza from the Nymphaeum appear the Corinthian porch, cloister (with altar in the centre) and gabled hall of the council chamber. To the right of this is a precinct containing a small temple (per-haps of Augustus), and on the extreme right appears the south end of the North Agora. The granary was the long building behind the council chamber (shown in the model as bisected by a street). Museum photographs.

57   Citadel of Pergamon, view from the south-east. Photograph by Max Hirmer.

58   Pergamon, model of citadel seen from the south; in the Berlin Museums. Museum photograph.

59   North-west corner of Great Altar of Pergamon, as restored in the Berlin Museums. The sculptured frieze is 7 ft 6 in. high; first half of the second century BC. Museum photograph.

60-61   Marble statue group of Galatian leader and his wife evading capture, in National Museum, Rome. Height 7 ft; copy of a Pergamene work of about 230 BC. Alinari photographs.

62   Great Altar of Pergamon, detail of battle of Gods and Giants. Museum photograph.

63   East front of Temple of Apollo at Didyma, Hellenistic era. Photograph by Max Hirmer.

64   Hill-top sanctuary of Hemithea at Kastabos in South-west Caria, restored view from the south-east by W. H. Plommer. The temple, dating to the second half of the fourth century BC, and similar to that of Priene, was strongly influenced by classical Athenian Ionic; but it is not certain that it had a deep frieze like that conjecturally shown in the drawing.

65   Coin portraits of Hellenistic rulers. British Museum photographs.
a. Battle of Alexander and Porus on the Jhelum 326 BC.
b. Seleucus I Nicator, ruler in the East 312–280 BC (from a coin of Philetaerus of Pergamon).
c. Philetaerus, governor of Pergamon (d. 263 BC), from a coin of Eumenes I.
d. Antiochus III, King of Syria 223–187 BC.
e. Demetrius, King of Bactria, invaded India about 184 BC.
f. Antimachus, brother of Demetrius, ruler in Bactria.
g. Mithridates VI Eupator, King of Pontus (coin of 75 BC).
h. Nicomedes IV, King of Bithynia (coin of 84 BC). In contrast to the animated portrait of Mithridates, this coin shows a ruler who was perpetually being harried by Italian business-men.

66–68   Theatre at Aspendus in Pamphylia, second century after Christ.

69   Aqueduct at Aspendus, of Roman Imperial times. It is mainly built of dressed stone, but brick and rubble are also used in the pressure towers

70–72   Sanctuary at Ba'albek (Heliopolis), mainly second century after Christ. Plates 70 and 71 show the flanks of the Great Court, Plate 72 the interior of the so-called Temple of Bacchus.

73–74   Ba'albek, little domed temple outside the great precinct.

75 Entrance pylon of South Agora of Miletus, restored in the Berlin Museums; second century after Christ. Museum photograph.

76 Artemis of Ephesus. This lifesize marble replica of the celebrated cult image of the Artemisium was discovered in 1956 in the Austrian ex- cavations on the site of the town hall of ancient Ephesus; it was originally gilded. The goddess' robe is adorned with carved animal figures, signs of the zodiac, and eggs (rather than breasts) symbolizing fertility. The tower- ing embattled head-dress is lost, but is known from other copies. Photo- graph provided by the Austrian Archaeological Institute.

The statue here illustrated seems to have been deliberately buried about 400 AD to safeguard it from fanatical Christians who were rifling the pagan monuments. A recently discovered relief, in which the effigy of this goddess appears in an assembly of the family of the emperor Theodosius, testifies that at this time Artemis was still venerated as the patron and pro- tectress of the city of Ephesus.

Index

Index

Index